EMBRACING PRODIGALS

Embracing Prodigals

Overcoming Authoritative Religion
by Embodying Jesus' Nurturing Grace

JOHN SANDERS

 CASCADE *Books* • Eugene, Oregon

EMBRACING PRODIGALS
Overcoming Authoritative Religion by Embodying Jesus' Nurturing Grace

Cascade Books
An Imprint of Wipf and Stock Publishers
199 W. 8th Ave., Suite 3
Eugene, OR 97401

www.wipfandstock.com

PAPERBACK ISBN: 978-1-7252-6406-9
HARDCOVER ISBN: 978-1-7252-6407-6
EBOOK ISBN: 978-1-7252-6408-3

Cataloguing-in-Publication data:

Names: Sanders, John, 1956–.
Title: Embracing prodigals : overcoming authoritative religion by embodying Jesus' nurturing grace / John Sanders.
Description: Eugene, OR: Cascade Books, 2020 | Includes bibliographical references.
Identifiers: ISBN 978-1-7252-6406-9 (paperback) | ISBN 978-1-7252-6407-6 (hardcover) | ISBN 978-1-7252-6408-3 (ebook)
Subjects: LCSH: Political psychology—United States. | Polarization (Social sciences)—United States. | God.
Classification: BL2525 .S240 2020 (print) | BL2525 (ebook)

Manufactured in the U.S.A.   JULY 17, 2020

CONTENTS

ACKNOWLEDGMENTS

I am grateful to a multitude of people who assisted me on this book. In particular, my wife, Jody, offered many good suggestions and, more importantly, she models the nurturing way of life. My friend Aaron Simmons has participated in countless conversations with me over the years. His wisdom has been of inestimable benefit. Several of my colleagues at Hendrix College deserve a shout-out for sharing their expertise with me: Jay McDaniel, Kiril Kolev, Robert Williamson, Leslie Zorwick, and Jay Barth. Bonnie Howe, Kevin Carnahan, Chris and Thea Spatz, along with two of my children, Mandie and Caleb, offered insights and encouragement along the way. I am grateful to a wide array of people who read parts of the manuscript and provided feedback: Brenda Colijn, Karen Winslow, Curtis Holtzen, Alan Padgett, Barry Callen, Dwight Erickson, Norrie Friesen, Josh Norris, Ginny Ahrens, Paul Kuan Richards, Colin Bagby, Devon Dundee, Andrew Fiser, Terri York, and Tricia Burris.

INTRODUCTION

PARENTS AND PRODIGALS

Jesus was a rabbi who liked to tell stories. One of his most famous stories is the parable of the Prodigal Son. This story sets the stage for this book so even if you are familiar with the story, please follow along. "There was a man who had two sons. The younger of them said, 'Father, give me the share of the property that will belong to me.' So he divided his property between them. A few days later the younger son gathered all he had and traveled to a distant country, and there he squandered his property in dissolute living. When he had spent everything, a severe famine took place throughout that country, and he began to be in need. So he went and hired himself out to one of the citizens of that country, who sent him to his fields to feed the pigs. He would gladly have filled himself with the pods that the pigs were eating; and no one gave him anything. But when he came to himself he said, 'How many of my father's hired hands have bread enough and to spare, but here I am dying of hunger! I will get up and go to my father, and I will say to him, 'Father, I have sinned against heaven and before you; I am no longer worthy to be called your son; treat me like one of your hired hands.'"

So he set off for home. While he was still far off, his father saw him and was filled with disgust and anger at the son. The father waited in the house. When the son arrived he said, 'Father, I have sinned against heaven and before you; I am no longer worthy to be called your son.' The father replied, 'You got that right. You are a disrespectful child whose way of life failed to honor me as the Ten Commandments requires.' The son said, 'Father, forgive me.' The father replied: 'If I forgave you and welcomed you back home I would be treating your sins lightly. Just as we cannot be soft on crime, I cannot pass over your sin. You subverted the social order God established. If I let you off free of charge that would undermine society. Divine justice requires you to get what you deserve. You must be punished and pay the price in order to satisfy my indignation and balance the moral books.' Then the son said to the father, 'please let me be one of your hired hands to pay for my sin.' The father agreed, saying, 'Exodus 21 allows for you to be a slave for the next six years. If you work hard in the fields, you can pay off the tremendous debt you owe to my honor. Do this well and you will earn my acceptance.'

When the older brother came in from working in the fields the father said to him, 'You are an upright son who honors me by obeying my authority. Your deviant brother returned today and I agreed to let him pay off his sin by working for us. Keep a good eye on him for me until his account is paid in full.'"

The first half of this story is the way Jesus told it but the second half is completely different.[1] Here is another version of the story which is also different from the one Jesus told. The first part is the same: the son receives his share of the inheritance, leaves home, and ends up in a desperate situation. He realizes that there is plenty of food at home so he makes the long trek back. While he was a long way off the father saw him, ran to meet him, and gave him a high five. The son said to his father, "After I departed my situation deteriorated so I decided to return home again." The father said, "It does not matter what you did, you are always okay with me. I always affirm what my children do and never make judgments about them. You know that I do not have expectations about how you live your life. I just accept you as you are." The father threw a party that night and when the older son came in from the fields he went into the house. When he saw his brother he said, "Everything is cool between us, welcome back." The party went well and they all had a wonderful time.

In the first adaptation, the father is very judgmental and makes the son earn his way back into the family. The words and actions of the father in this story make a lot of sense to us because this is how many fathers we know would react. The values and behaviors of the father in this account fit with what I call the Authoritative parent. Not only is this approach common in families, many Christians believe God operates just like the father in this version. They develop theologies and ways of relating in church life that manifest these values. In the second adaptation, the father makes no

---

1. I got the idea for this version from Robin Collins.

moral judgments. There is no need for forgiveness because the father makes no moral evaluations about the kids. Fewer parents practice what is called the Permissive parent approach.

The story Jesus actually told is at odds with both the Authoritative father and the Permissive father versions. The story Jesus told has the same first two scenes in which the son receives his inheritance, leaves, and ends up in a perilous situation. He said, "I will get up and go to my father, and I will say to him, 'Father, I have sinned against heaven and before you; I am no longer worthy to be called your son; treat me like one of your hired hands.'" Now is where Jesus' version of the story differs from the two told above. Jesus says the father saw the son a long way off and was "filled with compassion," not disgust and anger. The father ran to meet him instead of waiting in the house. The father embraced him and kissed him instead of making the son grovel at his feet. "Then the father said to his servants, 'Quickly, bring out a robe—the best one—and put it on him; put a ring on his finger and sandals on his feet. And get the fatted calf and kill it, and let us eat and celebrate; for this son of mine was dead and is alive again; he was lost and is found!'" When the oldest son came in from working in the field he heard music and dancing and so asked one of the servants what was going on. The servant said his father was throwing a party for the safe return of the younger son. The older son became angry and refused to celebrate. He sulked outside instead. When his father became aware of this, he went out of the house and pleaded with the son to come in and join the party. However, the older son thought the father was acting immorally. He replied, "Listen! For all these years I have been working like a slave for you, and I have never disobeyed your command. . . . But when this son of yours came back, who has devoured your property with prostitutes, you killed the fatted calf for him!" His father replied, "Son, all that is mine is yours but we had to celebrate because your brother was dead and has come to life; he was lost but has been found."

Three pieces of background information help us fill out what Jesus meant by this story. First, Jesus tells this story immediately after he tells two other stories about searching and finding lost items. In the first parable, a shepherd had a hundred sheep but one got lost. The shepherd went and found it and brought it home. In the second story, a woman had ten coins and lost one. She searched diligently until she found it. Jesus tells three parables about sheep, coins, and sons that are lost and then recovered. Second, Jesus told these stories in order to answer a question that religious leaders put to him: why did Jesus show acceptance and hospitality to sinners? The term *sinners* here has a very specific meaning. It means Jewish people who do not practice their religion the way the religious leaders expected them to. For example, they did not keep the Sabbath and were lax about other regulations that God had commanded. According to some religious authorities, Rabbi Jesus should not show acceptance to people who do not follow God until they first change their ways. Third, the request of the younger son to have his share of the inheritance was legitimate in ancient Judaism. However, to take it and leave the country was an outrageous act that cut him off from his family.

With this in mind, we are now in position to understand the ways in which Jesus' approach to people with problems differs from both the Authoritative and Permissive fathers.[2] In the Authoritative father version, the father, who represents God, cannot simply forgive and accept the child because he thinks justice demands that we get what we deserve. We must keep the moral books lest society fall apart. However, Jesus tells a very different story. The father does not wait in the house for the son to come and grovel at his feet. Instead, the father goes to meet the son, embraces him, and gives the son what he does not deserve. It is the son, not the father, who says the son is unworthy to be called a son. It is important to note that the father does not frame the situation in terms of disobedient children. Rather, the father frames the situation as the joy parents have when they find their missing child or when a child recovers from a life-threatening situation. By construing the situation as finding his lost son or surviving a life-threatening condition, the father sees the situation very differently than the Authoritative father does.

In Jesus' story, the oldest son, not the father, gives voice to Authoritative values when he frames the situation as dishonor and the need for judgment. That is why he accuses the father of being unfair and acting immorally. This son says the father is not acting like an Authoritative father should. The older son says the father should make the prodigal earn his acceptance. However, Jesus says God does not demand repayment or punishment in order to bestow divine acceptance. Rather, God lavishes acceptance and forgiveness in order to transform human lives. Ask yourself when you are most open to transformation. When someone condemns you and sternly tells you to shape up? Or, when you feel deeply and profoundly loved?

---

2. For an excellent account of the parable in terms of what it means to embrace others even while holding them morally accountable, see Volf, *Exclusion and Embrace*, 156–65.

Returning to Jesus' version, the older son refuses to go into the house and fulfill his social responsibility to help the father entertain the guests. In spite of this dishonor, the father goes out of the house to talk to the older son as well. He accepts this son as well and invites him to join the party. The story does not tell us whether the older son with Authoritative values accepted the invitation of the father with Nurturing values to enter the house.

In contrast to the Permissive version, Jesus does not say whatever the younger son does is okay. Jesus agrees that the "sinners"—those Jews not in proper relationship with God—have a problem. Jesus does make evaluations about their condition when he characterizes them as lost and dead. Their situation is dire and definitely not what God wants for them. The son is wrong because he rejected his "sonship" by cutting himself off from his kin. What he did was to "un-son" himself so he could not expect to be welcomed back as a family member. The best he could hope for was to become a hired hand. The Permissive father emphasizes acceptance without moral evaluation while the Authoritative father is all about moral judgment, not acceptance. The Nurturant father makes moral evaluations and uses welcome and embrace to transform the child. In common with the Authoritative father, Jesus wants these Jewish people to change their ways. In contrast with the Authoritative father, in order to bring about this transformation the father goes to them, welcomes them with open arms, and calls them his children. Though the son excluded himself from the family, the father never excluded him. God, according to Jesus, does not exclude these Jewish "sinners" because God's relationship with them does not depend on their moral performance. The son cannot undo the relationship because the father always kept the son in his heart. Though the younger son sought to un-son himself, the father makes it clear that the young man is his son when he tells the servants to dress him and put a ring on his finger (what servants did for family members). According to Jesus, God prioritizes forgiveness and family relationship over rule keeping. Of course, few of us have done exactly what the prodigal son did. Yet, Jesus tells the story to give us a fundamental model of how God relates to us.

WHAT THIS BOOK IS ABOUT

This book names two forms of religion—Nurturant and Authoritative— that have butted heads from the time of Abraham to today. These two ways of life have existed for thousands of years in families, religions, and governments. They are competing moral visions of life that are manifested in the way parents raise children, in government policies, and in religious teachings regarding how God deals with people. Teachers and coaches use these orientations when they seek to motivate people. Politicians use them to set policies ranging from crime to health care. During the past fifty years, polarization has greatly increased in the United States over an array of political and cultural issues. The key that explains this divide is the Nurturant and Authoritative moral visions. They represent two deeply opposed views of what constitutes a good person. Each approach believes it has the best set of values, practices, and attitudes for living life properly. Each side believes the stance taken by the other is wrongheaded.

The Authoritative, Nurturing, and Permissive types embody different sets of values that people live by. For instance, Nurturants prioritize traits such as acceptance, empathy, cooperation, perspective taking, and open-mindedness, and they support democracy. Authoritatives cherish obedience to rules, social order, individual responsibility, absolute certainty of the correctness of their views, and lean towards autocratic leaders. Permissive types favor tolerance, open-endedness, and minimalist structure. This book deals primarily with the Nurturing and Authoritative types for several reasons. Social scientists have focused their studies on these two for decades. In addition, the Gospels primarily depict people who follow the Nurturing or Authoritative ways of life. The Authoritative types were the ones who regularly challenged Jesus' values. Another reason is that in the history of Christianity and particularly in America today, the debates over doctrines and correct practices occur primarily between the Nurturant and Authoritative types. The core values in each view lead Christians to develop different theologies, ways of relating, and stances on social issues. Those with Authoritative values find it natural to affirm ideas such as penal substitution, hell as eternal torment, the Bible as a book of moral absolutes, and corporal punishment. Those with Nurturing values have different understanding of these topics.

The various chapters following lay out the key values in each model. These values motivate people to think and behave the way they do. Cognitive science informs us that much of our reasoning, including thinking about morality, is unconscious. The moral values in these two models, like an iceberg, go largely unnoticed by us yet they shape us in powerful ways. Even if you have not heard the names before, the Nurturing and Authoritative approaches will feel familiar to you. The reason why is that the models name icebergs—the value sets we experience in everyday life and the church.

There are two main claims in this book. The first is that authentic Christianity follows the Nurturing path of Jesus. Jesus came to turn us away from a way of life based on authority, tribalism, and getting what you deserve to one grounded in acceptance, grace, love, and forgiveness. Chapter 3 gives evidence that Jesus strongly taught and lived out the Nurturant approach to life. Time after time Jesus rejected the Authoritative approach with its tribal deity who did not forgive but, instead, demanded obedience in order to be accepted. There are scriptural texts that teach Authoritative values but Jesus largely ignores them. When he does mention Authoritative scriptural texts, he says they are wrong and puts his own Nurturant teaching in its place. In his handling of Scripture, he selects texts emphasizing a Nurturant God. Chapter 3 shows that there is Nurturant religion in the Old Testament that existed alongside Authoritative religion. God sought to move Israel from a fear-based, get-what-you-deserve religion, to one where love and grace were foremost. For example, Exodus 34:6–7 revises Exodus 20:5–6. The earlier passage said that people needed to obey the rules in order for God to love them but the latter passage changes it to say God will love them no matter what. Not everyone followed God's leading on this, however. Many people emphasized the Authoritative texts and forced the Nurturant texts to fit into the Authoritative mold. They taught that God loved only those who ate the right food, said the right prayers, and kept themselves free of the "contamination" from outsiders. First-century Judaism had both Nurturants and Authoritatives and Jesus sides with the Nurturants. He discloses what God is like and how God wants us to live. Jesus mines from the Nurturant veins of the Old Testament. He showed grace to Jews who did not practice the food laws and welcomed Gentiles. He sought to bring people more fully into the Nurturing life and invited those who lived by the Authoritative approach into a more nourishing way of life. He wanted to change how families and institutions relate to one another.

The second main claim is that the Nurturant approach creates a better world in which to flourish. Research in psychology and sociology demonstrates that people with a Nurturant orientation produce children who are more self-reliant, prosocial, possess greater psychological well-being, and have more secure and trusting relationships than do those with Authoritative values. States and communities with Nurturant values are safer, healthier, and better places to live. Chapters 1, 4, and 7 discuss these topics.

Authoritative types like to say that their way is the right way to live but the evidence clearly undermines their claim. Of particular interest is the significant body of social science research on people who believe in either a Nurturing or Authoritative God. The findings show that those who affirm a Nurturant deity have better mental health and more secure attachments than do believers in the Authoritative God. Chapter 4 shows that different Gods create humans in their image. What we think God is like matters greatly for our well-being and relationships.

The way we understand God also matters when it comes to things as diverse as what we believe about salvation, hell, how we handle religious questions, the purpose of moral rules, and the role of the Bible. Nurturant and Authoritative believers develop quite different beliefs about what Christianity is. For instance, those with Nurturing values see the Christian life as a pilgrimage and think that there are usually several good views on any particular doctrine. On the other hand, those with Authoritative values establish a fortress Christianity and enforce the single correct view on any topic. If you question the established view, they put you in stocks or exile you from the community. I used to wonder why the same groups of Christians lined up on different sides of debates about what God is like and the nature of atonement.[3] Now I see that the values inherent in each life orientation explain why some theological ideas make sense to one group and not another. Chapters 5 through 9 explore topics such as the atonement of Jesus, how the Bible functions in our lives, the cognitive styles we practice, what a moral life involves, and politics. The Nurturant and Authoritative cognitive models brilliantly illuminate the theological and political debates from atonement to what to do about income inequality. The different sets of values in each approach explain why Christians believe and relate the way they do. Many authors today write from the Nurturant orientation and identify some of the problems with the Authoritative orientation. Yet, none of them provides a comprehensive mapping of the iceberg underlying the doctrinal, moral, and political divides. This book furnishes a big-picture overview to help make sense of why family members and neighbors so strongly disagree with one another about what to believe, how to treat others, and how to vote.

Grasping these two models helps us in several ways. First, understanding what motivates people to arrive at different views enables us to

---

3. My scholarly publications discuss these ideas in more detail. Lists of my publications and versions of many of my papers are available at my website: drjohnsanders.com.

have fruitful conversations. We can talk to one another about our differences in a more informed way. Second, it will help Nurturant Christians live out their values more consistently. In recent decades, proponents of the Authoritative approach have been more proactive about framing theological and social issues in ways that fit with the Authoritative values. This is especially the case regarding the white evangelical subculture that has become strongly Authoritative. Even churches historically aligned with the Nurturant approach, such as the Wesleyan and Pentecostal churches, are succumbing to Authoritative values. A better grasp of what the Nurturing way of Jesus is about gives Christians the insights needed to develop doctrines and social policies in line with Nurturing values. Third, it provides an invitation to those influenced by the Authoritative way to change and walk in the path of Jesus instead. The New Testament as well as the early history of Christianity show that many people were deeply attracted to the Nurturing way of Jesus because of the way it changed how people related to one another. Nurturing Christianity was revolutionary in the way, for instance, that it cared for those suffering from plagues, because believers provided health care to even non-Christians.

Unfortunately, the Authoritative approach is a powerful siren call that shipwrecks many believers on the rocks of its moral vision. Repeatedly, believers have filtered and distorted the gospel of Jesus until they produced an Authoritative version of Christianity that gained wide acceptance. Those with Authoritative values have produced theologies about God, sin, and salvation that fit with the Authoritative model. They did this so well that it became a dominate form of Christianity. Today, we see the polarization between Nurturant and Authoritative religion in families and churches. In my experience, people are yearning for the Nurturing God Jesus revealed. We can improve our lives, our congregations, and even our governments via the Nurturing path. We thrive when we live out these values because God intended us to live this way.

Finally, this book is addressed primarily to Christians, but the Nurturant and Authoritative types are found in most religions. This book can serve as a guide for Jews, Muslims, and Hindus who want to develop nurturing forms of their religions.

The first chapter details what the Nurturant and Authoritative cognitive models involve. Chapters 2 and 3 discuss Jesus' teachings and other biblical texts supporting the Nurturing view. Chapter 4 shows that those who believe that God is Nurturing are better off psychologically and socially. The remaining chapters explore how the Nurturing and Authoritative approaches understand various theological and ethical topics.

1

MEET THE PARENTS

For many years, my wife and I disagreed about the best approach to child rearing. I thought it sufficient to clearly state the rules and expect our kids to obey them immediately and without question. My wife was more attuned to where each child was developmentally and sought to understand why they acted up at times. When they did act up my first thought was they were challenging my authority, whereas my wife wondered whether they were not feeling accepted and loved. It turns out that our two approaches to child rearing are quite common, both historically and around the world.

Below are four sets of characteristics in children. You may feel yourself torn between the options in each set. However, select the value in each pair you prefer. Which of the following qualities do you believe is more important for a child to have?

- Independence or Respect for Elders
- Good Manners or Curiosity
- Well Behaved or Being Considerate
- Self-Reliance or Obedience

Which ones did you select? If you chose independence, curiosity, being considerate, and self-reliance then you strongly embody the Nurturant parent values. If you chose respect for elders, good manners, well behaved, and obedience then you strongly affirm the Authoritative parent approach. Of course, as explained below, there are people who select some from each and so are a mix of these ideal types.

These four questions are the Rosetta Stone used by researches around the world to identify types of people. The questions occur in important surveys such as the American National Election Studies and the World Values Survey that studies hundreds of countries. Researchers use them to identify people who affirm the values and dispositions associated with the Nurturing and Authoritative approaches to life. The traits we prefer in children correlate to the type of vehicle you drive, the TV shows you watch, the types of pets you have, and the kind of coffee you drink.[1] More significantly, the responses tell us whether you are wary of outsiders, how you understand fairness, and whether you believe the world is fundamentally a good or dangerous place. The answers people give accurately predict their stances on issues ranging from health care to income inequality.[2] In fact, child-rearing preferences accurately predict fundamental orientations toward authority and the stances people take on many cultural and political issues.[3] The reason is that the characteristics we desire in children disclose some of our core values. They embody a deeply entrenched moral vision that guides us on the path of life.

Material on parenting styles identifies four types determined by the degree to which parents are (1) responsive (emotionally warm and accepting) and (2) demanding (holding children accountable to high expectations). My names for the types are Permissive, Nurturant, and Authoritative.[4] Permissive parents are unconditionally accepting, extremely lenient, and make few demands. They are highly responsive and have few expectations. On the other end of the spectrum are Authoritative parents, who are highly demanding and have a lower degree of responsiveness and acceptance. Between these two types are Nurturant parents, who score high on both responsiveness and demandingness. They couple high expectations with strong emotional warmth. Few parents fall into the fourth category: Disengaged parents who are neither responsive nor demanding.

---

1. For an easy-to-read overview of the findings, see Hetherington and Weiler, *Prius or Pickup?*

2. Barker and Tinnick, "Competing Visions."

3. Mockabee, "Question."

4. Diana Baumrind's threefold parenting typology is widely used in the field of child rearing. The names she uses are slightly different from those I use. She calls them Permissive, Authoritative, and Authoritarian. That is, her Authoritative is what I call Nurturant and her Authoritarian is what I call Authoritative. Her reasons for using "Authoritative" for those who are both highly responsive and demanding is quite understandable. However, this book uses the terminology commonly used in politics and sociology.

Researchers who focus on political and social issues focus on the Nurturant and Authoritative types rather than on the Permissive and Disengaged. This book does as well.

THE NURTURANT PARENT

Nurturing parents want children to become responsible and self-reliant as they navigate new situations in life. To accomplish this, they set high expectations and enforce standards while simultaneously providing acceptance and affection. Parents furnish structure, order, and predictability by establishing routines, managing children's schedules, and supervising peer associations. It is important to note that Nurturing and being an authority are compatible because Nurturant parents understand themselves as the authority in the home who sets and enforces the standards. Nurturing is not blind and is not an "anything goes" approach. Nurturing parents make evaluative judgments and confront wrongdoing. When the child does something harmful, the parents correct and discipline the child. The goal of discipline is restitution and reconciliation rather than retribution. Obedience arises from love and acceptance rather than fear of punishment. Parents are issue- and goal-oriented rather than focused on rigid obedience. Families are groups of people who rely on one another, so trust and accountability are crucial for them to function well.

As children mature, they are encouraged to exercise increasing independence in developmentally appropriate ways with the goal of becoming self-reliant. They should be able to think on their own, operating on their core values while negotiating new situations and problems in life. This means they may need to innovate and improvise rather than simply mimic the behaviors of the exemplars. Children are encouraged to ask questions in appropriate ways since independence of mind is valued. Parents are sensitive and open to suggestions from the child. They are flexible in how they enforce expectations and are willing to negotiate when children provide reasons. Changing one's mind in light of new information indicates one is willing to follow the truth and act responsibly.

The Nurturant approach recognizes that it takes teamwork, a village, to raise a child. Although the parents have ultimate responsibility, educators, neighbors, friends, clubs, and others play important roles in helping our children mature. Children need to learn to live together in families and communities. Consequently, learning to cooperate with others is a priority.

Parents seek to inculcate a sense of social responsibility in children to care for the well-being of others.

Political scientists and sociologists find the following characteristics associated with adults who affirm Nurturant values.

- Justice is primarily about making sure that all people have a solid opportunity to fulfill their potential in life. All should share the goods and services of society.

- Individuals need to be morally responsible for themselves as they live in community with others. Mature people have developed character traits that guide them as they relate to others. Trusting relationships and interdependence are important.

- Cooperation and social responsibility are core values. Social and public programs are investments in our communal life.

- Concern for others extends to those outside their immediate in-group.

- The emphasis on teamwork and community leads to a preference for democratic or shared governance in various institutions, including churches. They seek to ensure that all people have a voice. Even in settings where one person is ultimately in charge, leaders are sensitive to the interests of those who contribute to the organization or community.

- Though individuals have personal responsibility, systems play an important role in our lives. There are, for example, judicial, educational, and health systems that affect each of us. These networks, however, are not always fair to everyone, so sometimes the system can be a barrier to living out your potential.

- Nurturants place higher importance on emancipative values regarding personal freedom rather than social conformity. They respect the social and moral orders while acknowledging that human institutions are not perfect and may need to change.

- Some of the key values for this way of life include empathy for others, individual and social responsibility, dialogue, perspective-taking, cooperation, and tolerance.

THE AUTHORITATIVE PARENT

Parents who emphasize authority want children to become responsible people who live in obedience to the rules established by the legitimate authorities such as God, government, and parents. Parents manifest love to their children through high expectations and strictly enforcing compliance to them. When children disobey, punishment is direct and harsh behavioral control along with rejection (nonacceptance). Parents may withdraw love to instill fear of what happens when disobedience happens. They may also use guilt to motivate the child. When bad behavior occurs, the focus is on retribution rather than reconciliation. The punishment is coercive and often corporal in order to teach children the painful consequences of breaking the rules. Children learn obedience out of fear of punishment.

Authoritatives see the world as a highly competitive place so children have to learn how to succeed in the struggle against others. When children are coddled, they do not acquire the strength needed to survive in a dog-eat-dog world outside the home. The world is a dangerous place so children must obey the moral rules in order to avoid dangers. Parents prevent their children from spending significant time with those who do not share Authoritative values. According to this view, children are morally weak and require strict discipline in order to become morally strong. A morally strong person survives dangers, overcomes competitors, and gains the acceptance of those in authority. Unless they learn compliance, children will become wicked and undermine the social order.

Adults have the proper knowledge about how to live, so children should passively accept the rules of the adults. Questioning the rules shows disrespect for the authority who established them. Repeated obedience produces compliance. The emphasis is on strict control rather than fostering independence. When children challenge the parents' decisions, the parents threaten punishment. Like breaking a horse so that it complies with bridle and bit, parents must break the strong-willed child so that the child complies. When children ask for an explanation the parents give "Because I say so" as the only reason needed. They do not discuss the intended benefits to the child because that would encourage questioning and possible defiance. Parents are not open to suggestions from the child and they do not negotiate with them, as this would foster disrespect for authority. Parents rigidly enforce the expectations rather than being flexible. Changing your mind about something means you are a flip-flopper.

The Authoritative approach emphasizes self-interest. The focus is on the development of a single moral agent who follows external rules. Of course, children need to learn to live with others and the best way of teaching this is helping children learn that it is in their own self-interest to do what the authority dictates. Children become good people by learning that it is in their self-interest to obey. When each child individually follows the rules then home life flows more smoothly.

For many proponents of the Authoritative approach the person in charge of the family is the father. He is the primary authority and the mother is secondary. He has the responsibility to financially support and protect the family. He sets the rules and strictly enforces them by punishing the children when rules are broken.

Social scientific research associates the following characteristics in adults who affirm the Authoritative approach.

- Justice means getting what you deserve. If you follow the rules, then you deserve a reward. If you break the rules, then you deserve punishment. The amount of your reward is proportional to the amount you contributed. Emphasis is placed on law and order. When people do wrong, they must pay for it. In addition, no individual or group receives preferential treatment over others, regardless of historical circumstances (such as slavery).

- Those who earn money deserve to keep it. Social programs take money away from those who deserve it. Those in authority should not give benefits to the undeserving since that rewards weakness and coddles people. The government should not be a "nanny state." It should not interfere with the initiatives of the strong.

- Moral traditionalism is very important. Legitimate authorities put the moral rules in place and obeying them is in our self-interest. The moral traditions provide clear right and wrong instructions for how to live. The moral standards are absolutes. Questioning or revising the absolutes undermines authority. Typically, God is the authority who gave the absolutes. Since it is entirely inappropriate to challenge God, these rules are not negotiable in society.

- In order to maintain the social and moral orders in society, clear boundaries are required along with intolerance towards social deviants who cross the boundaries.

- Concern for others is restricted to one's tribe (in-group) of ethnically and religiously like-minded people.

- Individuals need to be self-sufficient and take care of themselves. When everyone does this then society will flow more smoothly. The educational and economic structures provide each person with a level playing field to succeed in life. If you are not doing well, do not blame the systems, blame yourself. Inequities in education and the work place are the fault of individuals either being lazy or bad people. Either way, they lack the moral strength to do well. Authoritatives are usually disgusted when minority groups protest against social structures. They believe the fault lies with the individuals, not the institutions. It is wrong to categorize individuals and groups as "vulnerable." Rather, they are "weak," so coddling them only keeps them from becoming strong and successful.

- It favors autocratic leaders in institutions, including churches. A strong leader knows what is best for everyone, takes charge, and is in control of the situation. Many believe that just as fathers are in charge of the family, so males should be in charge of our churches and government.

- Some key values for this way of life include respect for authority, obedience, moral strength, moral traditions, and giving people only what they deserve.

THE BREAKDOWN

Sixteen percent of Americans are strongly Authoritative (answer all four questions the same way), while 26 percent answer three of the four on the Authoritative side.[5] Strong Nurturants comprise 13 percent of Americans while 19 percent select three of the four Nurturant responses. The remaining 26 percent are "mixed" in that they choose two Nurturant and two Authoritative answers. In the last fifty years, the numbers of those favoring Authoritative and Nurturant values have grown while the population of mixed has shrunk. This helps explain the increasing polarization in society and in churches.

---

5. See Hetherington and Weiler, *Prius or Pickup?*

THE NURTURANT APPROACH PRODUCES BETTER QUALITY CHILDREN

Although both the Nurturant and Authoritative parenting styles are coherent and each has millions of people who practice it, the empirical research shows that the Nurturant style produces better results than either the permissive or Authoritative styles.[6] These results do not depend on social or racial background or the marital status of the parents. Furthermore, studies show the Nurturant approach superior in countries around the world, including China, Australia, Pakistan, and Argentina to name but a few. This is important because these counties are quite diverse in many significant respects. For example, some are collectivist while others are individualist cultures. Yet, the Nurturing style is superior in these cultures as well. Studies also show that highly effective educators, coaches, and administrators use the Nurturant approach. Children raised by Nurturing parents and educators exhibit greater degrees of self-reliance, prosocial behavior, confidence in social settings, motivation to achieve, cheerfulness, self-control, and less substance abuse.

To live optimally requires us to develop competence in some important areas. We need to cooperate and commune with others while also having the ability to assert ourselves and express constructive dissent. A healthy community needs individuals to work together, which requires concern for others, friendliness, trust, and the ability to comply with the norms of the group. On the other hand, a healthy community also needs people who can take initiative, have self-determination, and resist groupthink. Children raised by prototypical Nurturant parents are more likely to possess these traits in optimal ways.

Children raised in strongly Authoritative families are less able to chart their own moral course (they need someone to tell them what to do in new situations), have less of a conscience (they need an external moral guide), are less respectful towards those who are different, and have less ability to resist temptations.[7]

---

6. For the empirical evidence on the superiority of the Nurturant approach for child rearing, see the following literature, noting that in child-rearing literature many researchers use the term "Authoritative" for what I call "Nurturant" (see note 3 above). Larzelere et al., *Authoritative Parenting*; Bun et al., "Effects"; Lamborn et al., "Patterns"; Baumrind, "Influence"; Abar et al., "Effects."

7. Lakoff and Johnson, *Philosophy*, 327.

Overall, it is best is to have high expectations (demanding) and provide emotional warmth and support (responsive). The prototypical Nurturant parent style is neither too hard nor too soft, but gets it just right, as in the story of Goldilocks and the three bears. Those who score high on both expectations and emotional closeness are the best at producing more competent and well-adjusted children. There are variations of both the Nurturant and Authoritative styles who do a good job of raising competent children, but not as well as those raised by prototypical Nurturant parents. These are: (1) parents who are moderately demanding and highly responsive and (2) parents who are highly demanding and moderately responsive. These are not as optimal as parents who are both highly demanding and highly responsive, which is the prototypical Nurturing approach.

COGNITIVE MODELS

The Nurturant and Authoritative ways of life are "cognitive models" that explain people's attitudes and behavior. The models are shorthand for the sets of values and the moral vision people live by. George Lakoff's *Moral Politics* applied these models to a wide array of issues in American society. Many political scientists, sociologists, and psychologists use these models, though not everyone uses the names Nurturant and Authoritative to identify them.[8] For example, two sociologists noticed a pattern in data from the 2005 and 2007 Baylor Religion Survey. The researchers found statistically significant patterns to the way people responded to two questions about (1) what God is like and (2) what God does (or does not do) in our lives. They discovered that Americans have four main views of who God is and how involved God is in our lives. The insightful book, *America's Four Gods: What We Say About God—and What That Says About Us*, discusses the findings.[9] Two of the views of God they found are the Benevolent (Nurturant) and Authoritative. The Baylor Religion Survey shows correlations between the people who hold each view of God and issues such as climate change, same-gender marriage, the role of government in helping people, and attitudes about wealth and poverty. The incredible explanatory power of the models sheds a lot of light on different kinds of Christians.

---

8. Other names for the Authoritative approach are disciplinarian, authoritarian, and strict father. For a survey of the research on these two models, see Jost, "End."

9. Froese and Bader, *America's*.

When people read the summaries of the Nurturant and Authoritative ways of life, they find them quite familiar and intuitive. These moral visions are deeply entrenched in our thinking. That is why they feel familiar to us. The models, like most of our thinking, operate unconsciously, yet they shape us in powerful ways. Like an iceberg, they go largely unseen, remaining mostly underwater. However, as soon as we focus on them, these two approaches to life make sense and sound very familiar to us because they name core values we take for granted. That is why the Authoritative version of the Prodigal Son story easily makes sense to us—it fits a life orientation we already know.

In order to understand how our two models function we need to understand a bit about what makes them meaningful to us.

METAPHORICAL PARENTING

In Christianity, it is common to think of God as the parent and believers as a family. We often think of the government as a parent and the nation as a family.[10] Family life is one of several domains we use to reason about society. When we understand God as a parent, we are using a mental tool called conceptual metaphor.[11] We use metaphors to understand things so often that we often fail to notice them. Sometimes, people say, "Oh, God as parent is *just* a metaphor." However, metaphors are incredibly powerful tools of reasoning and not mere rhetorical devices. Some examples will make this clear. In English, we use a variety of metaphors to understand love. We say "Frank is nuts about Mary." When we do this, we conceive of our experience of love in terms of insanity. Sometimes we feel that love overrules our mental faculties. We also think of love as a nutrient (food) when we say, "Her love sustains him" or "She is starved for affection." We construe love as fire ("She is burning with devotion"), as magnetism ("They are strongly attracted to each other"), and as natural forces ("He was swept off his feet by her"). A prominent way to conceive of love in English is the metaphor of a journey. We use our experience of traveling to understand love as distance traveled ("Our relationship has come a long way"), as decisions ("We came to a crossroads in our relationship"), as obstacles overcome together ("We

10. For an explanation of these metaphors, see Lakoff, *Moral Politics*.

11. The information here is based on cognitive linguistics. See Sanders, *Theology*, for a fuller explanation and how it applies to Christian thought.

had some bumps along the way"), and as the need to repair the relationship ("We need to get back on track").

These are just some of the metaphors used in English to understand the multifaceted experience of love. It is very important to notice that these metaphors are being used to reason about love. We are thinking about love in terms of insanity, nutrients, and journeys. These are not rhetorical devices but ways of reasoning. According to conceptual metaphor theory, we have language that is literal, but it is quite limited. For example, we can say of a love relationship that there is literally a lover and a beloved. However, we want to say more than this, so we think of love using areas of life such as nutrients, physical forces, and journeys. Metaphors are an ordinary yet extremely important tool in our mental toolbox. A key feature of metaphors is inference and the different metaphors for love have different entailments or logics to them. If we construe love as insanity, then we are not responsible for our actions. This is quite different from conceiving love as a journey where we are responsible for our actions. The gift of each metaphor is that it helps us grasp an important aspect of our multifaceted experience of love. The limitation is that no single metaphor says everything we wish to say about love.

Biblical writers used a wide array of metaphors to understand what God is like and what our relationship to God is. If God is a shepherd and we are sheep, then the divine shepherd has many responsibilities to care for us but there are not many expectations for how we are to behave. However, if we think of God as our spouse then there are mutual expectations and responsibilities for both parties. Thinking of love as insanity or God as shepherd say some important things about love and God but conceiving of love as a journey together or God as our spouse yields many more insights for living. The metaphors we use shape our values and behaviors in significant ways.

Each of these points about metaphor is important. When we think of God as a parent or the government as a parent, we are using a common human experience to understand our relationship to God or the government. Parenting is a rich domain to draw from because it provides plenty of deep and meaningful ideas about the behaviors and values we should enact. Humans have thought of God and government as parents for thousands of years. Of course, though parenting is a particularly useful way to understand God or government, parenting does not say everything we want to say about these subjects. However, the parenting metaphor is incredibly illuminating and explains a lot of what we are experiencing today.

PROTOTYPES

At the beginning of the chapter, you selected four characteristics you prefer in children. Some people select the four nurturing characteristics, some choose the four authoritative traits, while others select some of both. The Nurturant and Authoritative ways of life each have a prototype such that when you meet someone with those traits you think that person is a "genuine" Nurturant or Authoritative. Prototypes or exemplars are another important mental tool for reasoning. Researchers find that when asked to give an example of a bird, any bird, the vast majority of Americans select something like a robin or blue jay. For Americans a robin is an exemplar of the category *bird*. They have feathers, fly, have a particular size and shape, and eat certain types of food. A robin or blue jay has these prototypical features and so functions as the "center" of the category *bird*. Of course, there are other types of birds, such as hawks, ostriches, and penguins. Such birds share several of the features, or family resemblances, with robins but they do not necessarily share all of the same features. When humans think of categories of things we tend to think in terms of a central example and then allow for less representative examples. For Americans, robins are a central example of the category bird. People consider some birds closer to the center and other birds further away from the center. Owls, for example, are birds but less representative than robins. Yet owls are closer to the center (better examples of birds) than ostriches and ostriches are better examples than penguins. Penguins are "strange" birds, which is why they are towards the periphery of the bird category.

This means that many of our categories have gradations and variations in them. We have "radial" categories with a clearly identified central example and then as you radiate outward, away from the center, we have less and less representative examples of the category. Take the category *Christian*, for example. Jesus is the central example, the paragon, and then we would place people such as the apostles and Mother Teresa close to the center. Radiating outwards from them would be people considered good but not as great examples, such as John Wesley. We understand the category *Christian* as a continuum from the best exemplar to less and less representative examples.

The same is true when we think about Nurturant and Authoritative parents. Each of these types will have an ideal with prototypical features. There will also be gradations of both kinds of parents. Some people are not strongly Nurturant so they share some, but not all, features of the exemplar. They are like owls to robins. There is an ideal of the Authoritative orientation and then less representative examples who share some but not all of the characteristics of the prototypical Authoritative. As a result, we must not think that every person identified as a Nurturant or Authoritative parent has all the features of the ideal types. Yet, they will share a family resemblance and so will have tendencies to value the same sorts of things as the prototype.

In addition, it is important to keep in mind that it is possible for people to apply the Nurturant value set in one area of life and use the Authoritative set in another area.[12] For instance, a schoolteacher may use the Nurturant approach at home but employ the Authoritative approach in the classroom. In the *Harry Potter* series, Harry's aunt and uncle become his legal guardians. Their parenting styles differ between Harry and their biological son, Dudley. They deal with Harry in strongly Authoritative ways and are extremely permissive towards Dudley.

We use prototypes when we evaluate views other than our own. We naturally see things through the lenses of our ideal type. For instance, Authoritatives often accuse Nurturants of being indulgent and going easy on kids when they misbehave. They think that the Nurturant or Permissive approaches fail to discipline their children. This is true of Permissive Parents. However, Nurturant parents discipline their children and work hard to correct bad behavior. Yet, it does not seem so to the Authoritative Parent because according to their ideal, if one does not punish children exactly the way they do, then one is not disciplining at all. They believe only their approach makes people strong and upholds the moral order. For instance, an Authoritative might say of a president who does not inflict harsh punishment on another nation that the "parent" is not protecting the children (our nation).

The *Harry Potter* series provides an illustration of these contrasting approaches to discipline. Professors Dumbledore and Umbridge deal with Harry quite differently. Dumbledore welcomes Harry's questions and does not see them as a threat to his authority. He is patient with Harry's anxiety

12. In addition, the exact ways that Nurturants and Authoritatives apply their core values can vary somewhat within and across cultures.

yet challenges him to see that situations are sometimes more complex than they seem on the surface. Professor Umbridge, on the other hand, does not allow the students to question her or the textbooks since they are the authorities. The students are to memorize the lessons and she forbids questions. When Harry challenges what the Department of Ministry says about the Dark Lord, she calls Harry's words "lies" and makes him write "I will not lie" until his hand painfully bleeds the words. Church leaders, teachers, and government officials live out these same two approaches.

CONCLUSION

The names Nurturant and Authoritative are recent, but the ways of life and values in each model have existed for a very long time. Both types are found in the Bible and appear in the history of Christianity. A wonderful example of this comes from the twelfth-century church reformer and spiritual director Bernard of Clairvaux. He criticized the leaders of monasteries "who wish always to inspire fear" among the monks and nuns in their charge. Instead, he implores those in authority to follow Jesus who nurses us from his breasts. "Learn that you must be mothers to those in your care, not masters; make an effort to arouse the response of love, not that of fear; and should there be occasional need for severity, let it be paternal rather than tyrannical. Show affection as a mother would, correct like a father. Be gentle, avoid harshness, do not resort to blows, expose your breasts: let your bosoms expand with milk not swell with passion."[13] Bernard concludes by saying that fear causes Christians to flee from the authorities when they make a mistake instead of running to them as to the bosom of a mother. Correction, he says is better accomplished by nursing love than by the fear-based approach. Genuine authority, he says, operates in Nurturant, not Authoritative ways.

Each life orientation leads to different theologies, leadership structures, and ways of relating. The following chapters elaborate these differences. We will see that the two types arrive at very different understandings of, for instance, what God is like, atonement, and the purpose of the Bible. We are still debating the two models in contemporary America and the polarization between them is growing. Social scientists use these two models to explain what is going on in society. This book explores how these two orientations operate in Christianity. The cognitive models have huge

13. Cited in Bynum, *Jesus*, 118.

explanatory power that helps us better understand why Christians disagree on fundamental issues. The core values underlying our debates, like an iceberg, are substantive and powerful.

The next chapter looks at what Jesus taught and how he related to people.

2

THE NURTURING JESUS

I was at a theology conference listening to a scholar criticize one of my books. The theologian said that a problem with my approach was that I began with Jesus to know what God was like. He said it is wrong to begin with Jesus because, though he was God, he was also human so Jesus could not be our model for God. God, he said, was sovereign (a micromanager), full of glory and power, enforcing the divine will on everyone. Obviously, Jesus was not this way. I about fell off my chair. This theologian was using his Authoritative view of God to discount Jesus as the best revelation of what God is like. However, the New Testament writers emphatically say that if you want to know what God is really like, then look at Jesus because "He is the reflection of God's glory and the exact imprint of God's very being" (Heb 1:3). Paul says that Jesus is "the image of the invisible God" (Col 1:15) and "in him the whole fullness of deity dwells bodily" (Col 2:9). When the disciple Philip asked Jesus to "show us the father," Jesus replied, "Whoever has seen me has seen the father" (John 14:9). John declares that Jesus is the "glory" of God, full of grace and truth (John 1:14). In his teachings and actions, Jesus made known what God is like. This chapter examines Jesus while the next chapter looks at other biblical texts about God.

GOD SHOWS LOVE AND ACCEPTANCE

First, and foremost, Jesus shows us that God loves us. God so loved the world that God sent the son of God to us (John 3:16). Divine love motivated the mission of Jesus. A few years ago, a pastor asked me to review his notes for a sermon on the attributes of God. His notes did a good job on God's wisdom, holiness, and power. I told him that what he said was fine but what he left out was troubling—there was nothing about love in the notes. He was shocked that he had forgotten to mention God's love so when he gave the sermon he began with a confession that his original message had omitted this key attribute of God, but he was going to highlight it now.

The Judaism of Jesus' day contained both Nurturant and Authoritative varieties. Hillel, the most famous rabbi of the previous century said to love peace and care for everyone. Once, a person came to him and said he would convert if Hillel could teach him then entire Torah while he stood on one foot. So, while the man stood on one foot Hillel said, "What is hateful to you, do not do to your neighbor. That is the whole Torah; the rest is the explanation." In a similar vein, someone asked Jesus to state the most important teaching in the Scriptures. He said to love God with everything you have and to love your neighbor as yourself. Jesus selects Deuteronomy 6:5 and Leviticus 19:18 to sum up the entire Old Testament (Matt 22:36–40). On another occasion, Jesus told his followers to "love one another as I have loved you" (John 13:34). Loving God and loving others is the heart of true religion according to Jesus.

What about people with whom we do not get along? Exodus says "When you come upon your enemy's ox or donkey going astray, you shall bring it back" and says we should help the animal of those "who hate us" (23:4–5). Jesus develops these sorts of scriptural texts when he says, "You have heard that it was said, 'You shall love your neighbor and hate your enemy.' But I say to you, love your enemies and pray for those who persecute you.'" He says that loving your enemies shows that you are a member of God's family (Matt 5:43–45). To understand how ridiculous this sounded to his listeners, put yourself in their situation. The Romans, with their pagan gods, occupy your country and exploit you and everyone else for the well-being of the elites in Rome. For example, a Roman soldier could legally require you to carry his gear for one mile but no farther. Nobody wanted to do this humiliating service to support the oppressors. However, Jesus says if a soldier forces you to carry his gear, then carry it for two miles (Matt 5:41). What Jesus said to do runs counter to Authoritative teaching, which said to resist, or better yet, kill the Romans. After all, God hates Romans. They are the enemy of God. In fact, they are the ones that deserve torture and crucifixion, not us. Jesus said to love and treat others the way we want to be treated (Matt 7:12). This was revolutionary against Rome but not the kind of revolution that Authoritative types wanted.

The Authoritative types said that Jews who failed to live the way God commanded did not deserve hospitality or acceptance because God is against them. However, Jesus shows acceptance to them when they do not deserve it and he forgives without demanding that they change first.[1] On one occasion some Authoritative types asked Jesus why he showed acceptance to Jews who did not keep the moral rules God had given in the Bible (Luke 15:1–2). How can Jesus embrace tax collectors who work for the evil empire, or sinners (Jews who do not live the way God said)? They did not keep the Sabbath and present offerings in the Temple. They did not even bother much with attending the synagogue on Saturdays. The religious leaders who confronted Jesus believed God was going to punish such lawbreakers. They are confounded that Jesus shows hospitality to sinners by eating with them. That is not what a "good" rabbi should do because a proper rabbi operates by Authoritative values. However, Jesus sides with the Nurturant form of Judaism and explains himself via three parables. In each story, something important is lost and God searches to find it. Jesus frames the situation as a case of lost and found rather than lawbreaking, as the Authoritative leaders did. In the parable of the Prodigal Son (discussed in the introduction), Jesus agreed that such Jews were out of proper relationship with God. The question was how best to change their lives. In the story, Jesus says the Jewish father lavishes acceptance and hospitality on the troubled boy in order to change his life for the good. The father provides transformative love.

Jesus' teaching on love, acceptance, and forgiveness went against the grain of the Authoritative religious leaders of his day. Yet he was not a Permissive parent, either, who says whatever the child does is fine. He agrees that Jewish "sinners" have problems and do not live the way God desires—he says they are "sick" and he wants to restore them to health (Matt 9:12). After accepting people, he sometimes told them to go and sin no more. When he forgave sins, he implies that the person had done something wrong. To forgive acknowledges that a wrong has occurred and it means that it is not okay to treat others that way. Genuine love evaluates what we do and seeks what is best for others. Jesus says that God is aware of wrongdoing on the part of the Romans as well as Jews. However, he says that God shows love

---

1. For how the Bible depicts God's acceptance and grace, see Jipp, *Saved By.*

and forgiveness in order to empower people to change the way they treat others. Jesus teaches the Nurturant way of life.

Jesus showed love and acceptance to those who were not part of his in-group. There were those who did not worship as he did, ate foods he did not eat, did not look like he did, and did not share his core values. Yet, he reaches out to such folks and embraces them. He lovingly interacted with both the oppressed and the oppressors. Jesus healed the servant of a Roman military officer, a member of the colonizing oppressors (Matt 8:5–3). He ate with a large crowd of tax collectors, people who supported the oppressive regime and who were considered enemies by nationalistic Jews (Luke 5:29). He went to the house of one of the leaders of the Pharisees and accepted the hospitality of a meal (Luke 14:1).

The religious laws of the day excluded certain women but Jesus shows acceptance to them. A Jewish woman who suffered from a hemorrhage wanted Jesus to heal her. She touched Jesus as he passed by and Jesus asks who touched him. She is silent because she knows the religious rules. According to Leviticus, she was to be isolated from others because whomever she touched became ritually impure and unable to worship God. Frightened, she kneels before Jesus who, instead of condemning her, blesses her and grants her peace (Luke 8:43–48). On another occasion, Jesus and his disciples are traveling through Samaria. Many Jews considered Samaritans religious apostates and did not associate with them. Jesus asks a Samaritan woman for a drink of water and she is surprised because using her cup would ritually contaminate him. Jesus accepts her by entering into conversation with her and seeks to change her life (John 4:4–26). There is also a story about a Canaanite woman. The Canaanites were the everlasting enemies of Israel in the Old Testament. She causes a scene by shouting at Jesus and his disciples. She wants Jesus to heal her daughter. Jesus tells her that his mission is for the Jews but she persists and replies that even the puppies get to eat the crumbs that fall from the table—can't she just have a crumb? Jesus accepts her, says she has wonderful faith, and heals her daughter.

The jaws of the disciples dropped to the ground during these encounters. They were astonished that Jesus showed love to outsiders and to those who eventually killed him. According to Authoritative values, Jesus loved all the wrong people: sinners, tax collectors, Samaritans, and Roman military officers. Jesus should not have shown acceptance to them until they had first changed their ways. Jesus teaches that God loves the in-group and the out-groups and shows indiscriminate love to all before they change their ways. God's grace is given to everyone. The early followers of Jesus will use these teachings to transform the idea of the "people of God" from that of an ethnic group with its tribal God to one that includes all nationalities and tribes.

All this ran counter to what the religious Authoritatives believed. For them, religious purity was necessary for Israel's national identity to safeguard against paganism. Eating the proper foods and following correct temple worship were essential to retaining God's favor. The only true people of God are those who follow the rules. Those who did not keep Sabbath, the dietary laws, and male circumcision were obviously not acceptable to God, according to Scripture. The Authoritative types repeatedly confront Jesus. They want to know if he flies the flag of God. Does he affirm the temple of God, the Sabbath of God, the moral code of God, the food of God, and the tribe of God that sets them apart from the pagans? Does he follow the path of God or not? Jesus replies that he is bringing about a divine revolution that sets aside these boundary markers of who is in and who is out. Of course, this was blasphemy to the Authoritatives. They could not bring themselves to think God worked this way because it went against their core values.

Those with Authoritative values try to limit the in-group God accepts to those who have the proper beliefs and institutional affiliation. They think God does not love outsiders so they should not love the outsiders either. One such person raised this very point with Jesus. He agreed with Jesus on the preeminence of loving God and loving your neighbor. However, he asked, just who is my neighbor? Is it limited to those who worship, behave, and eat like me? In response, Jesus tells the parable of the Good Samaritan. Of course, according to the Authoritatives in the audience, there was no such thing as a "good" Samaritan because God rejected them. They were not included in God's covenant because they do not have true temple worship or Scripture. However, Jesus says that God draws the boundaries differently than the Authoritatives. Jesus teaches that to love Israel's God means to love the "neighbors" that are not part of the tribe.

There is judgment and exclusion by God but not for the reasons that Authoritative types think. Jesus tells a parable about a king whose son is getting married. The servants travel to invite people to come but those invited shun the invitation and some even assault and kill the servants. The leaders who believe that the only good Roman is a dead Roman and those who think God detests those who fail to properly keep God's rules, are the ones who refuse to come to the wedding. The king's son in the story is Jesus. Those sent the wedding invitations think that what Jesus teaches about God is crazy and opens the floodgates to pagan encroachment and the destruction of God's people. If that is what God is like and Jesus is the king's son, they want no part of that kind of Messiah. They want a nationalistic Messiah who will destroy the pagan enemies of God. They want a Messiah who will punish the Jewish sinners and the Romans. They want a God who gives people what they deserve. However, Jesus says God has Nurturing values. Jesus works to develop a nurturing people and a better society than that offered by the Authoritative way. In the parable, the king invites everyone to the banquet. Everyone has the king's acceptance and favor. The only ones excluded are those who exclude themselves by refusing God's hospitality.

MORAL ACCOUNTING

When someone invites us over for a meal or helps us move to a new apartment we usually think, "I *owe* them one." It is natural to be grateful for the gift of help, but why do we conceive of the situation as one of debt? The reason is that many cultures, for thousands of years, have understood certain types of moral actions in terms of financial accounting. That is, they metaphorically think of morality as accounting.[2] In accounting, if I borrow money from you, then I am in your debt until I repay it. If I use a credit card, I temporarily borrow money to pay for an item and thus accrue a debt to the bank. I have a financial obligation to pay back the money I have borrowed. When I complete the payments, there is no more debt because the financial books are balanced. We need not understand moral actions metaphorically as financial transactions. Yet it is very common. That is why when someone gives us a gift we think we owe them something in return. When someone does something good to us, we believe that we should do something equally good for them. When someone does something harmful to us, we believe that we should do something equally harmful to them in return. Retribution is exacting the proper punishment for the harm they caused. In financial transactions, people get what they deserve until the books are balanced. In moral accounting, people get what they deserve until the moral books are balanced. In both, it is about getting what you earned.

---

2. For more on how we use metaphors to think about morality, see Sanders, *Theology*, 139–52.

Jesus, however, rejects the negative side of moral accounting. In the Sermon on the Mount, he mentions the teaching in the book of Exodus (21:24) regarding an eye for an eye and tooth for a tooth. When someone injured another, then the same degree of harm was to be done to the offender. However, Jesus says, "You have heard that it was said, 'An eye for an eye and a tooth for a tooth,' but I say to you, Do not resist an evildoer. But if anyone strikes you on the right cheek, turn the other also; and if anyone wants to sue you and take your coat, give your cloak as well; and if anyone forces you to go one mile, go also the second mile . . . You have heard that it was said, 'You shall love your neighbor and hate your enemy.' But I say to you, Love your enemies and pray for those who persecute you" (Matt 5:38–44).

Jesus also teaches that God gives people what they do not deserve. For instance, in the parable of the Vineyard, the owner finds workers who agree to the standard daily wage (Matt 20:1–16). They begin in the early morning. Throughout the day the owner continues to hire more people (at midmorning, noon, midafternoon, and at late afternoon). Everyone assumed the owner used moral accounting to determine how much to pay each worker. Those who worked all day should receive the daily wage and those who worked only a few hours would get much less. However, the owner gives everyone a full day's wage! When someone complains that this is "unfair," he replies that if he wants to be ridiculously generous and give people what they do not deserve that is his decision to make.

New Testament scholar N. T. Wright says that Jesus' teachings regarding judgment are about how Israel's God is visiting the people in the person of Jesus, the Messiah.[3] God is calling people to forsake the nationalistic understanding of the Messiah who hates both the Romans and Jewish sinners. They expected God to come to Israel and destroy both the pagans and the Jew who did not properly follow God's rules. Then, God would vindicate (show to be in the right) those Jews who had properly worshipped God and lived within the biblically mandated boundaries of Sabbath, circumcision, and food laws. However, Jesus proclaims that in him, God is visiting Israel and he intends to begin a revolution that will change the world.

In other words, Jesus says they must give up their Authoritative values and adopt Nurturant ones. Jesus tells his followers not to exact retribution and revenge in order to balance the moral books. He teaches that God is incredibly generous and gives people more than they deserve. This is

3. Wright, *Challenge* and *Jesus*.

revolutionary and runs against the mighty stream of Authoritative values. Psalm 103:10 says God "does not repay us according to our iniquities." Jesus agreed, saying God does not "repay" our wrongdoing with equal harm to us. Instead, God "repays" our evil with grace and love. This is unfathomable according to our moral accounting schema and Authoritative approach to life. In fact, according to these values, the way of God in Jesus is immoral. However, this is exactly what Isaiah means when he says God's ways are not our ways (Isa 55:8). God forgives when we would not. Jesus calls a spade a spade—he calls people "evildoers" when they harm others (Matt 4:39). He does not say they are innocent. Yet, he opens his arms to embrace them and offers forgiveness in the hope that reconciliation comes about and their lives transformed. In the parable of the Prodigal Son, the older brother complains that the father should not throw a party for the son who has harmed the family. Instead, it is the older son who *deserves* the party because he has "always obeyed" the father. According to the Authoritative way of life, God should not embrace the wrongdoers until they show moral improvement. However, Jesus says that God's grace does not depend upon moral performance.[4]

JESUS IS THE TRUE AUTHORITY

Jesus said that all "authority in heaven and on earth has been given to me" (Matt 28:18). Jesus is the true authority but he does not behave in an Authoritative way. He redefines what it means to be a leader and wield power. He exercised authority by washing the disciples' feet (John 13). When the disciples debated which of them would have the highest rank in Jesus' government once he was crowned king, Jesus rebuked them. He said that it is typical for kings to "lord" their power over others but in his government things are different because the one who serves others is actually the greatest (Luke 22:24–27). Jesus is the true authority figure who identified with idolaters, sinners, and the ungodly. This is not the way leaders with Authoritative values behave. But Jesus is the pioneer who blazed the trail for us to follow (Heb 2:10; 12:2). Jesus embodied what genuine authority is about.

The evil one has taken humans captive and twisted our minds and hearts so that we do not live in nurturing ways. Jesus exercised leadership and authority when his self-giving love dethroned the evil one who ruins human lives (Phil 2:15). Jesus has shown us that the rulers and powers of

4. See Volf, *Exclusion and Embrace*, 85.

this age cannot separate us from God's love (Rom 8:38–39). Jesus has rescued us from captivity to return us home to God. Jesus is the new Moses who leads us out of bondage from the evil regime. In Luke 9, Jesus goes up a mountain with Peter, James, and John, and while he prays, his face glows. When Moses came down from meeting with God his face glowed as well (Exodus 34:29). In this story, Luke wants to make a key point but English readers seldom get it. Moses and Elijah appear and talk with Jesus about his pending "departure" in Jerusalem (9:31). Luke is not referring to a flight Jesus must catch. Rather, the word *departure* is the Greek word *exodus*. Jesus is the new Moses leading a new exodus from our bondage to the evil one. In Matthew, just as Moses had given the Torah (instructions) on Mount Sinai, so Jesus gives his instructions (sermon) on the Mount. Jesus gives his commandment to his people: love one another as I showed you (John 13:34). The climax of the exodus story was not the giving of the law in chapter 20 but the divine presence coming to dwell in the tabernacle (portable temple) in chapter 40. John says that the word of God became human and lived among us (John 1:14). The word *lived* here is the word for the tabernacle. John is saying that Jesus is the new tabernacle in which God's presence dwells among the people.

Jesus is the new Moses who leads a new exodus, establishes a new covenant, and inaugurates a new reign of the presence of God. Jesus is the authority who discloses what God is truly like: a father who embraces a wayward son, a king who forgives those who owe him money, an employer who pays workers more than what is due them, and a master who washes feet. He told his followers to reject the negative side of moral accounting—an eye for an eye. Instead, they are to love those who harm them. He accepted the outsiders: the pagans and sinners. He rejected the boundary markers of religious purity used by the Authoritative types of his day to identify the true tribe of God. Jesus was a Nurturant authority figure.

Nonetheless, those with Authoritative values find ways to fit Jesus into their moral vision. Puritans in early America emphasized the religion of the Old Testament. They sang little about Jesus, did not think his teachings very important, and his example was thought to be impractical. Jesus was important to them for one thing: he died as punishment for their sins to save them from hell. Otherwise, he was quite irrelevant to their lives.[5] Authoritative congregations continue to limit the importance of Jesus to his atoning death. Another common move is to highlight a few texts that seem

5. See Prothero, *American Jesus*, 44–45.

to affirm Authoritative values and use them to overturn all the Nurturing type texts such as those discussed above. It is fascinating how often the image of Jesus as hospitable to the ungodly is challenged by Authoritatives who say, "But Jesus chased the money-changers out of the temple with a whip" (John 2:15). They use this story to set aside the teachings about forgiving others, turning the other cheek, and the golden rule. They interpret Jesus' action to mean that God hates sinners and punishes those who do not keep to the strict rules. I agree with N. T. Wright that in this story Jesus deliberately selects an action that is full of symbolic meaning.[6] Jesus delegitimized the priesthood and their nationalistic goals. The brief disruption of temple operations by Jesus symbolized what was going to happen to the temple if the leadership failed to embrace Jesus' way of relating to the pagans. The nationalistic leaders persisted and the Romans destroyed the temple in 70 CE. Jesus did talk about judgment and he gave warnings for people to change their ways. These kinds of actions are consistent with the Nurturing approach.

Some people agree that Jesus taught the beatitudes, forgave sinners, accepted outsiders, and humbly washed feet. However, they interpret the book of Revelation and some other texts to mean that when Jesus returns he will be full of spite and hate for his enemies. He will round them up and torture them forever in hell. When Jesus returns, he will behave very differently than when he lived in Palestine. I guess such folks think that Jesus is serving time in heaven and when he gets out, he will be a changed man. I find it ludicrous to believe that the Jesus who forgave those who tortured him on the cross is going to change his ways.

Christian tradition and song call Jesus the prince of peace and the friend of sinners. He welcomed outsiders and forgave those who killed him. According to Jesus, this is what God is like. This is what divine hospitality, love, and justice look like.

Les Misérables wonderfully depicts Jesus' values. The criminal, Jean Valjean, is a bitter man just released from prison. He has no food or shelter. The bishop takes him in, gives him a meal and a place to sleep. The bishop showed him mercy but instead of being thankful, Valjean steals the silver plates from the bishop's residence and flees in the darkness. The next day the police catch him and bring him to the bishop. The bishop could have said, "I gave you a chance but you rejected grace so now you will be punished." Instead, the bishop does the unexpected and tells the police that

6. Wright, *Challenge*, 67.

Valjean did not steal the items since the bishop had given them to him. The bishop goes further and says Valjean forgot to take the candlesticks, so he puts them in his sack. Valjean cannot believe this for it runs counter to the way people have treated him all his life. So he asks the priest to explain what he is doing. The bishop says, "Jean Valjean, my brother, you no longer belong to evil, but to good. It is your soul that I buy from you; I withdraw it from black thoughts and the spirit of perdition, and I give it to God."[7] The bishop calls Valjean "brother" to indicate inclusion into God's family. The bishop heaps grace upon grace to the criminal, beginning the process of transforming Valjean's life. Jean then reflects upon his hatred for those who put him in prison for stealing bread and about how he had lived according to "an eye for an eye." He begins to give up his hate and becomes a person who loves and helps others as the bishop had done to him. Showing grace to others does not guarantee people will change. Valjean's bitterness towards the Authoritative justice system could have continued. Yet, Jesus says that if someone harms you seven times a day and then repents seven times, we are to forgive the person each time (Luke 17:4). Jesus said to go beyond forgiving seven times, but to forgive seventy-seven times (Matt 18:22). Forgiveness, mercy, grace, and acceptance are to be the distinguishing characteristics of the Jesus community.

7. Hugo, Les Misérables, 102.

3

GOD IS LOVE

Mary's letter described a series of gut-wrenching events during the past seven months. In August, she was at the gravesite with a friend whose husband had died after a seventeen-month struggle with leukemia. While standing under the canopy in the cemetery she thought to herself, "Where is God in all this?" It just seemed wrong for God to take a thirty-year-old man away from his wife and young daughter. Just before Christmas, another friend told her that her that the hospital sent her four-year-old son home since the second bone marrow transplant had failed. He died ten days later. Then, on Valentine's Day, Mary found out that her pregnancy had miscarried. A well-meaning Christian told her: "Well, we just have to believe that God has a plan and, somehow, your miscarriage is part of that plan." Mary wrote me, "I think God has a plan to redeem the world through Jesus, but I don't think taking my baby who never even made it to the heartbeat stage, let alone into my arms, even though I waited, prayed, and in the end pleaded for a whole year, has anything to do with the Plan. If it does, I'm not sure I want to be part of it."

Mary went on to thank me for publishing books on divine providence that helped her understand that God was not running around killing babies, children, and fathers in order to teach people lessons.[1] Over the years, I have received many hundreds of letters and phone calls from people around the globe expressing thanks for showing them a more helpful understanding of who God is and how God works with us. Many people have said that their

---

1. See Sanders, *God Who Risks*, and Pinnock et al., *Openness*.

belief in God was on the rocks until they discovered it was okay to believe in a God who was not to blame for the tragedies they had experienced.

THE NATURE OF LOVE

The New Testament book of 1 John says, "God is love" (4:16). According to the Baylor Religion Survey, 85 percent of Americans believe that "loving" describes God well. Yet, they differ about what love means. In particular, they disagree about how strict or forgiving God is and whether or not God's love extends to outsiders. So what is divine love like? John 3:16 says that God loves the "world," which includes everyone, not just the insiders. The book of 1 John says, "let us love one another, because love is from God; everyone who loves is born of God and knows God" (4:7). The passage goes on to say God loved us before we loved God, which is why God sent Jesus. God initiates love to the world. The Apostle Paul writes that God loves the weak, the ungodly, the sinners, and enemies (Rom 5:6–10). That is the same message Jesus gave. We cannot do anything to get God to love us any more than God always has. That is a revolutionary message.

Yet, some people try to limit God's love for the "world" to the "elect," the ones God chooses to receive grace. This is like a parent saying, "I love my family" and then secretly loving only some of the children. The Franciscan priest Richard Rohr says another way to limit God's love is common in the church: God will only love us after we change.[2] If you behave correctly, then God will love you. This is the Authoritative understanding of love. Benjamin Corey adopted some older children and asks us what would we think if he had said to them, "I love you but if don't love me back the way I want and if you don't perfectly follow my instructions, I'm going to torture you forever."[3] Though most people recoil at this, many Authoritatives believe God is like this. Norman Wirzba says, "Think how much people have been hurt by the image of a vindictive God poised and happy to punish and inflict pain. This is not the God of love" because it is "diseased rather than healthy, dirty rather than clean, degrading rather than nurturing."[4] The Authoritative view distorts what God is really like and twists the good news into "I will love you if . . ." However, the true God loves us, warts and all, and shows us grace and forgiveness that empowers us to change.

2. Rohr, *Divine Dance*.

3. Corey, *Unafraid*, 30.

4. Wirzba, *Way of Love*, 97.

1 Corinthians 13:4–7 provides further characteristics of love. It says love is patient and kind. It is not envious, boastful, arrogant, or rude. It does not insist on its own way. It is not irritable or resentful. It does not rejoice in wrongdoing, but rejoices when the truth is lived out. Love bears all things, believes all things, hopes all things, and endures all things. If this accurately describes love and "God is love" (1 John 4:16), then God is like this.

God has high expectations for how we live our lives. To bring this about God is patient and kind with us. God does not boast, "I'm the greatest" or say "it's my way or the highway." Instead, God puts up with us when we do wrong and works to correct us. God believes in us, which gives us the confidence to follow God's leading. God has faith in us—seen in the fact that God entrusts many responsibilities to humans. God hopes that divine patience and acceptance will empower us to be reconciled to God. God hopes that in the future our communities will exemplify divine love more fully. God practices faith, hope, and love. God is the exemplar of love, showing us how it is done.

The previous chapter discussed moral accounting: repay a good deed with a good deed and repay a harmful deed with a harmful deed. Jesus rejected doing harm to others (Matt 5:38–41) and the New Testament writers reinforce the same message. "Do not repay evil for evil or abuse for abuse, but, on the contrary, repay with a blessing" (1 Pet 3:9; see also 1 Thess 5:15; Rom 12:17). We break the cycle of retribution by showing mercy and forgiveness. The same point is made in the description of love in 1 Corinthians. The NIV translates the end of 13:5 as love "keeps no records of wrongs." But keeping records of wrongs is paramount for Authoritatives so that people receive exactly what they deserve.

The Greek and Roman philosophers taught that showing mercy was a character defect and was immoral because it means giving someone what they do not deserve. If people do not earn good treatment, then providing unearned help makes them dependent and weak. Early Christian teaching and practice swam against the strong Authoritative current of their society by affirming a Nurturant ethic. In the early centuries, people were attracted to the Christian way of life because the Jesus community loved those beyond their family and religion. One way that Christians manifested love was caring for the sick. During a fifteen-year plague in the second century, around a quarter of the population of the Roman Empire died. Many died due to lack of even basic health care. People abandoned family members for fear of getting the disease. The pagan priests and Roman officials fled the cities. The pagan gods were not known for their mercy, so why should those in charge care? However, Christians provided medical care for all, risking their own lives even for nonbelievers. Roman society had little concern for the poor, the weak, the sick, or prisoners. After all, the moral philosophers had said such folks did not deserve help. Christians got the reputation of going against the Authoritative grain of society. They fomented a revolution of love and mercy.[5]

WELCOME INTO GOD'S FAMILY

God, like the Nurturing parent, is both highly responsive and highly demanding. God's acceptance and emotional warmth come first, inviting people into the divine love. God displays acceptance of wayward people via a number of metaphors. God considers us members of God's family. The Apostle Paul says that the Holy Spirit motivates us to address God as "*Abba*," which is "papa" in English—a term of endearment, expressing emotional warmth and closeness (Rom 8:15; Gal 4:6). Paul says that we should not be fearful of God since God relates as a devoted, caring, and forgiving parent. In the home, God goes into Jesus' wardrobe and dresses us in the clothes of Christ (Gal 3:27). People in the community thus see us wearing the same apparel worn by Jesus. In addition, God changes our status from being "aliens" to citizens in God's country (Eph 2:19). Each of these metaphors stirs powerful memories in me due to experiences with our three adopted children from India. We welcomed them into our family along with our biological children. All of them called us Mom and Dad. Two of our adopted children were older children. Shortly after they arrived, I remember taking them to a shoe store where they got to select their own pair of shoes. They were shocked that we could afford to buy shoes from a store! We clothed them with the same kind of clothes worn by our other children. Finally, we experienced a ceremony in which they went before the judge who changed their status from aliens to American citizens. These events were important for our family and they are powerful metaphors for how God relates to us.

God says we belong to the divine family, clothes us with divine apparel, and makes us divine citizens. In light of these changes, God expects us to live a new way of life. Divine acceptance motivates us to adopt God's values. God becomes the exemplar whom we imitate in our lives. The New

5. See Stark, *Triumph of Christianity*.

Testament writers believed Jesus lived a life that corresponded to what God is like. That is why Christians "ought to walk just as he walked" (1 John 2:6). God has high expectations for us and uses love to empower us to live in a more excellent way—the way of Nurturing love (1 Cor 12:31).

GOD IN THE OLD TESTAMENT

When I discuss these ideas with students, it never fails that some will say that the God of the Old Testament is completely different from the God of the New Testament. They think the God of the Old Testament is highly judgmental, punishes people for trivial infractions, and only cares for the insiders who scrupulously obey God's rules. In short, they believe the God of the Old Testament is strongly Authoritative while the God of the New Testament is strongly Nurturing. Personally, I think this conclusion is quite incorrect. Yet, I admit that there are texts written from the Authoritative perspective. There are passages that depict God as incredibly judgmental, picky, and unforgiving. Some texts depict God as commanding genocide against entire people groups and others where God destroys large numbers for disobedience. Some Scriptures emphasize purity laws about who is acceptable and who is contaminated. One of the Ten Commandments says that God exercises conditional love; God punishes those who hate God and God loves those who are obedient (Exod 20:5–6).

Yet, there are also many Old Testament passages that depict God as loving, merciful, and forgiving.[6] In fact, some biblical writers revise and even reject what other biblical writers said (more on this in the chapter on the Bible). For example, one of the Ten Commandments claims that God's love was conditional upon following the rules. However, Exodus 34:6–7 radically revises this statement by declaring that God will love Israel in spite of their sin. In short, it revises the text from an Authoritative to a Nurturing approach. Another example of change occurs when the prophet Isaiah rejects a statement in Deuteronomy. Deuteronomy 23:1–3 says "No one whose testicles are crushed or whose penis is cut off" or "those born of illicit union" and "no Ammonite or Moabite shall be admitted to the assembly of the LORD. Even to the tenth generation." In other words, these types of people cannot ever have a relationship with the true God forever. Yet, Isaiah 53:3–8 singles out "foreigners" and "eunuchs" and says that they are

---

6. There are many more biblical texts for a Nurturing God than are discussed here. See Sanders, *God Who Risks,* and Fretheim, *God and the World.*

welcome to participate in the worship of God. For Isaiah, God welcomes people from different ethnic backgrounds as well as those with disabilities. Again, we see Nurturant values supplanting Authoritative values. The previous chapter gave examples of Jesus making this same move: selecting Nurturant texts to support his case while ignoring the Authoritative texts.

Though some of the Old Testament affirms an Authoritative approach, some of it is Nurturing. Exactly how much of the Old Testament fits into each view is not my concern. Let us begin with the story of the Exodus since it contains the laws that are so important to Authoritative religion. Note that God first liberated Israel and then God offered them a special vocation—to be a vanguard of people who treated one another the way God wants (Exod 19:4–6). God did not say, "If you obey me, then I will liberate you from Egypt." No, God saved them, put them on an "eagles' wings" flight out of Egypt, and once they were safe, then God offered them the vocation to be a special kind of witness for God in the world. Grace and mercy came first, followed by the offer of vocation that involved rules for community formation. God did not say, "If you follow the rules, then I will love and accept you. No, acceptance came first. God shows love to Israel but not because she has any special virtues to deserve divine favor (Deut 7:7–8). In fact, God loves Israel even when she acts immorally (Hos 11). When the people blow it big time by worshipping the golden calf, God declares that they have broken the covenant agreement to carry out God's vocation in the world. God tells Israel to proceed to the promised land but God will not go with them. God had said to build a tabernacle (tent) and the divine presence would dwell in the midst of the people. God cancels that plan. Ultimately, however, God forgives the people and restores the covenant with Israel's special vocation (Exod 34), the tabernacle is constructed, and the divine presence fills the tabernacle—God goes with them (Exod 40).

One of the most important texts in the Old Testament regarding the nature of God occurs in this story after the people break the covenant in the golden calf incident. After several dialogues with Moses, God discloses that God "is compassionate and gracious, slow to act in anger, abounding in lovingkindness, and forgives iniquity and transgression" (Exod 34:6–7). Yet, the passage goes on to say that God will by no means clear the guilty but will visit the iniquity of parents upon children and grandchildren. Commentators disagree about how to interpret this tension in the text. Some say it means that though God forgives, God still exercises just judgment, while others say the editors of Exodus could not agree about whether God is fundamentally Nurturant or Authoritative. Regardless, it is fascinating to look at how other biblical writers interpreted and used this passage. Fourteen other biblical writers quote this description of God, indicating how important it was to other biblical authors (e. g., Psalm 86:15; Joel 2:13). Thirteen of the writers quote only the part about God's nurturing qualities—grace, unbounded love, and forgiveness—while omitting the part about visiting the iniquity of the parents on the grandchildren. Only one author (Nahum 1:2–3) quotes the part about not clearing the guilty and omits the part about grace and forgiveness. So, we see that thirteen of the fourteen biblical writers who refer to Exodus 34 use it to advance a Nurturant view of God.

A common theme in the Old Testament is that God cares for those who are easily taken advantage of in society. The Scripture repeatedly uses widows, orphans, and aliens as examples of such people. Widows and orphans lacked a male provider while aliens were ethnic outsiders. The God of Israel is one who seeks "justice for the orphan and the widow, and who loves the strangers [non-Israelite residents], providing them food and clothing. You shall also love the stranger, for you were strangers in the land of Egypt" (Duet 10:18–19). Israel was to show mercy to those who did not "deserve" it. Leviticus is a book of purity laws that separate and exclude people for things such as flaky skin or wearing a garment made of two different materials. In the midst of these regulations it says, "You shall not take vengeance or bear a grudge against any of your people, but you shall love your neighbor as yourself" (Lev 19:18). And just in case you are tempted to limit "neighbor" to your tribe, a few verses later it says, "The alien who resides with you shall be to you as the citizen among you; you shall love the alien as yourself" (19:34).

Many biblical texts depict God as responsive to our prayers and open to our questions. The prayers of people can affect what God decides to do. For instance, Abraham negotiated with God (Gen 18:19–32). God does not shut Abraham down but allows him to have his say. God is patient with him. Jacob "wrestled" with God and God changed his name to "Israel," which means "wrestles with God" (Gen 35). God approves of those who wrestle with God. That is not the way an Authoritative God works with humans.

God and Moses have a number of memorable encounters in which Moses questions God. One of these occurs in the burning bush story. God tells him that God has heard the cries of the Israelites and wants to liberate them from oppression (Exodus 3). This is wonderful news. Then God informs Moses that God is delegating responsibility to Moses to go to Pharaoh. Moses is not interested in returning to Egypt. Instead of immediately obeying God, he gives God five objections to what God just said. In response to Moses's questions, God does not say, "Because I said so!" Rather, God responds to each objection with the reassurance that "I (God) will be with you." God does not force Moses to comply. God then tells Moses that the elders of Israel will believe that Yahweh, the God of Israel, has commissioned him. However, Moses objects, "What if they don't believe me?" God does not respond as the Authoritative God would by saying, "Look, I'm the one in charge and I know what I'm talking about." Instead, God gives Moses three signs to perform in the presence of the elders "so that they may believe that I appeared to you" (4:5). Moses's fifth reply is to tell God to get somebody else to do the job. At this God gets angry with Moses but instead of punishing him God modifies the divine plan to allow Aaron to do the public speaking instead of Moses. In response to Moses's five objections God is patient with Moses and employs flexible strategies to meet Moses's felt inadequacies. That is what a Nurturing God does.

About three dozen times in the Bible God is said to "change the divine mind" and these are often the result of humans negotiating with God. In fact, changing the divine mind becomes part of ancient Israel's confession of what God is like. God is said to be gracious and compassionate, slow to act on anger, abounding in lovingkindness, and one whose mind can be changed (Joel 2:13; Jonah 4:2). Of course, God does not simply accept every human request. There are biblical stories in which God denies an entreaty. The important point here is that just as Nurturant parents are open to input from their children, so is God. God listens to the input of humans and is open to persuasion. This is a sign of strength, not weakness.

GOD PLAYS JAZZ

Since God is responsive and open to prayers and questions, and since God loves us in the way described in 1 Corinthians 13, then God is patient and kind with us, guiding but not insisting "my way or the highway." This means that God does not micromanage people.[7] Instead, God's love delights in improvisation, with give-and-take. People like to say that "everything happens for a reason," meaning that God dictates every detail of what happens. However, humans have free will and do not always live in ways that God

7. For a full explanation of this, see Sanders, *God Who Risks*.

would like us to. God provides goals and directions but does not control our free will. God empowers others and delegates responsibility to them. God invites us to collaborate with God to build a better world. Yet, God does not wear overpowering fragrance or force us to watch ten episodes in a row of God's favorite TV show. Instead, God solicits our cooperation and empowers us. God has overarching goals but does not operate with a blueprint dictating how everything is to go. In fact, because God chooses to work through us, God employs flexible strategies for achieving divine goals, as God did with Moses. Instead of rigidly following a prewritten script, God resourcefully devises alternative scenarios by working with what is available at the time. God operates like a jazz musician, using a recognizable melody, but adding a great deal of improvisation in response to the other players. In addition, as with jazz, God encourages other band members to take a riff to put their own stamp on the song. God does not hoard the spotlight but takes delight in sharing it with others. Inviting our input means that God takes the risk that we mess up the music. Yet, even then, God does not give up on us but seeks to get the song going in a helpful direction again.

This portrait of God coheres nicely to the Nurturant values discussed in chapter two. God is both emotionally warm and responsive, on the one hand, and has high expectations, on the other. God expresses love and acceptance that empower us to live out divine expectations. God established a structured creation for the flourishing of creatures. God calls us to work collaboratively—to be part of a team—in order to fulfill the full potential God sees for every person. God is open to our questions, prayers, and desires. God employs flexible strategies that take the desires of others into account instead of demanding God's own way. God is love and exemplifies the characteristics of love as delineated in 1 Corinthians 13.

In sum, God is wise and resourceful in working with us when obstacles arise. God is faithful and perseveres to accomplish divine goals. In addition, God is forgiving when we fail and works to reconcile us to God. God does correct us but does so in a goal-oriented way—to restore the relationship. God does not punish for the sake of the rules or divine honor. Rather, God corrects in order to restore fellowship. God's love does not depend upon our obedience to divine commands. The God of Jesus and the God described in many parts of the Bible manifest Nurturing values.

THE AUTHORITATIVE GOD

The portrait of God painted in this and the previous chapter is quite different from that produced by people with Authoritative values. For them, God is highly demanding but not affirming. God expects humans to obey the divine commandments promptly and without question. Respect for divine authority comes first. When creatures properly honor God, then God shows acceptance to them. We must not sully the divine honor. Divine approval is conditional upon following the God-given rules. God shows love after people obey. Justice means getting what you deserve. If you are obedient then you are rewarded with good health and material comforts. If you disobey then you earn punishment. Wayward people must learn the "fear of God" by suffering the consequences through punishment. We need retribution for breaking the laws to restore order. Fear of divine punishment teaches obedience. To be a morally good person is to obey God's authority. Humans acquire moral strength from repeated rewards and punishments. The entire fabric of society is jeopardized when we do not obey. The world is a dangerous place and we avoid these dangers by strictly adhering to the divine moral code.

In the Authoritative version of the parable of the Prodigal Son told at the beginning of this book, the father is indignant when the son returns home. He believes that the son must pay for his failure to live according to the code of the father. The son must be punished and receive what he deserves. People need to become morally strong and this does not happen when they are coddled. The father withholds his acceptance and excludes the son from the family until he pays his debt to the father and society. If the father welcomed him back as a family member, forgave him, and celebrated his return, then he would leave the moral books unbalanced. It would reward bad behavior and fail to reward the obedience of the older son working in the fields. It would undermine society.

God is not responsive to creatures. God is the one in charge and so operates unilaterally. Only what God wants counts. God issues the directives and does not take kindly to questions. When people question God, the proper response is "Because I said so!" Negotiating with humans would undermine respect for divine authority and encourage defiance. God is closed to what others want. God never changes the divine mind, as that would indicate weakness. God has no need to be flexible or adjust divine plans. Prayers change us. They never affect God. It is hubris to believe God listens to us. Many years ago, after hearing my explanation that our

36

prayers can affect God, a well-known theologian pointed a finger at me and asked, "Who do you think you are to advise God?" This nicely captures the stance of the Authoritative approach to Christianity: we are supposed to be compliant, quiet, and do what God says without question. What about the numerous biblical stories in which the prayers and questions of people move God to change the divine mind? The proponents of the Authoritative God acknowledge such texts are in the Bible but claim that the passages only "seem" to teach that God is affected by what we say or do. If we can affect God, then they claim that God would be less than perfect and fail to be the ideal authority figure, completely in charge. God would thus fail to be a proper deity.

Many Authoritative believers think that God is "in control" means God micromanages creation. Everything in life happens for a reason. God has a blueprint and orchestrates everything that happens to fulfill the divine glory. Generally, people get what they deserve. If they are obedient and play by the rules, then they are prosperous. If they disobey then God punishes them with diseases, natural disasters, loss of a job, or other bad things. Disobedience must not go unchecked so God punishes us to teach us lessons, which instill fear in us so that we will not repeat our noncompliance. Disasters such as hurricane Katrina and events such as the 9/11 attacks are God's "wake-up call" for Americans to clean up their society.[8] Such ideas are not new. In the Middle Ages Europeans interpreted the Black Death as divine punishment for displeasing God and they attacked minority groups, such as Jews and "witches," who they believed were the ones breaking God's social mores. The minority groups were obviously displeasing to God since they did not fit in. People called them moral contaminants. Fear of them resulted in efforts to expunge them from the community in order to end God's punishment on the entire society.

The Authoritative God exercises authority like a Caesar, not Jesus. The God who says, "It is my way or the highway" does not love according to 1 Corinthians 13. The God who does not listen to us or forgive us is not the God of the Bible. The domineering, unforgiving, micromanaging, Authoritative deity lacks key Christian values and is not worthy of emulation. Part of Jesus' mission was to liberate us from the twisted view of God preached by Authoritatives.

8. See Froese and Bader, *America's Four Gods*, 27–29 and 133–35.

TRINITY

Christianity affirms that the one God eternally exists "in three persons." We have no experience of what it is like to be such a being so the doctrine is a mystery. Yet, the doctrine is important for a number of reasons. One of these is that the Trinity helps us understand what it means to say, "God is love." God has forever existed as Father, Son, and Holy Spirit. These metaphors speak of relationship and so relationality is internal to God. The Father, the Son, and the Holy Spirit eternally love one another. Prior to the universe, the godhead experienced relationships of love. Early Christian writers spoke of the mutual indwelling (*perichoresis*) of Father, Son, and Holy Spirit. The members participate in the lives of the other by lovingly giving and receiving. This means that God is fundamentally relational and loving. The way God relates to creatures manifests the same kind of love shared between the members of the Trinity.

The doctrine of the Trinity implies that there is one God but there is difference in God because the Father is not the Son and the Son is not the Holy Spirit. The very being of God is a unity in difference. The Father does not demand sameness but delights in the difference of Son and Spirit. Richard Rohr speaks of the Trinity as the "divine dance" and says that the dance is one of Nurturing love. "Trinity says that God's power is not domination, threat, or coercion, but instead is of a totally different nature. . . . *All divine power is shared power, which should have entirely changed Christian politics and relationships.*"[9] To be like God, power sharing should be a mark of Christian communities.[10] The Father shares power with the Son and the Spirit instead of "lording it over them." In other words, the Trinity is the source and paragon of Nurturing love. The very being of God manifests the Nurturant, not the Authoritative, way of life.

As one might suspect, there are those who construe the Trinity in Authoritative ways. For instance, some high-profile evangelical theologians defend the view that the Son and Spirit are "functionally" subordinate to the Father.[11] The Father is in charge and the other members of the Trinity obey. These evangelicals want to find a pattern of subordination in the godhead so they can defend their subordination of women to males in the home and church. The early church had some clergy who affirmed the subordination

---

9. Rohr, *The Divine Dance* (location 1917). Italics in original.

10. See Volf, *After Our Likeness*.

11. See Giles, *Trinity*.

of the Son to the Father but the second ecumenical council condemned "subordinationism" as heresy in 381. Nonetheless, it is not surprising that some contemporary Authoritatives seek to uphold this teaching because it fits so well with the Authoritative moral vision.

CONCLUSION

God is watching you captures the Authoritative approach in which God has laid out the rules and meticulously keeps track of our compliance. *God is watching out for you* gets at the Nurturant values of God's concern for us. Though some biblical texts paint an Authoritative God, the overall portrait of God is one of nurturance and benevolence. The God of Israel, known as Yahweh, is called the "God of gods and the LORD of lords, the mighty and awesome deity" (Deut 10:17). What does Yahweh do with this exalted status? The next verse says Yahweh brings about justice for orphans and widows and shows love to aliens in the land. God is indeed exalted and uses this lofty status to care for those exploited by the powerful. Similarly, Jesus did not regard equality with God as something to cling to but, instead, "emptied himself" of status to become a human (Phil 2:6–7). Jesus is Lord, the authority over the church, but he shows how to be a proper authority by doing things such as washing the disciples' feet. What is God like? The previous chapter on Jesus and this one show that the Christian God loves us and relates to us in Nurturing, not Authoritative, ways. Your view of God has real consequences for life. That is the topic of the next chapter.

4

DIFFERENT GODS CREATE US
IN THEIR IMAGE

For more than a decade, I regularly filled the pulpit in a variety of church-es for several months at a time while they waited for a permanent pas-tor. Regularly parents would say to me, "I want to thank you for coming. I have enjoyed your messages but even more, my children have never wanted to come to church before. They love your sermons." The main reason why people responded so positively is that most of the messages were about the Nurturing God portrayed in biblical narratives. People in these congre-gations cherished hearing about the God who listens to their prayers and loves them, warts and all. They longed to learn more about a God of grace and mercy who showed them how they should live in community.

Paul said, "Be imitators of God" (Eph 5:1) and this has been a popular notion throughout Christian history. The idea is that God is an exemplar upon whom we should model our lives. The way God treats us is the way we should treat others. Thus, different types of Gods are going to produce different kinds of people. Richard Kearney writes: "Tyrannical Gods breed tyrannical humans."[1] Likewise, a Nurturant God seeks to create empathetic, forgiving, and caring people. Gods make us in their image because we imi-tate the God we believe in. This chapter discusses research that shows that believing in a Benevolent God produces people with healthier relationships and better mental health than those who believe in an Authoritative God.

---

1. Kearney, *Anatheism*, 147.

FINDINGS FROM THE RESEARCH

The vast majority of Americans believe in God but their views of what God is like differ tremendously. The Baylor Religion Survey asked people a range of questions about social issues and their beliefs about God. The book, *America's Four Gods*, uses this data to identify four different understandings of God in America.[2] The questionnaire scores people according to (1) how involved they believe God is in their lives and (2) the extent to which they believe God judges people in this life or the next. Two of the views of God, the Benevolent (Nurturant) and Authoritative, are widely held by Americans. Both views believe God is involved in people's lives but they differ on divine judgment. The other two views of God in the book are the critical and distant Gods. Neither of these views believes God is presently involved in our present lives. Proponents of the critical God think God rewards and punishes only after death. The distant God is not really an agent with a mind or will but more like a force such as gravity. The distant God is not as popular as the Benevolent and Authoritative Gods but it is the fastest growing view today.[3] Of course, there are more than four views of God and some people have a mix of the Nurturant and Authoritative views. Sometimes people use one view when dealing with a particular type of issue and switch to another view when facing a different matter. This book seeks to help people more fully follow the Benevolent God. Perhaps an encouraging sign is that 97 percent of Americans who say they believe in God "as described in the Bible" also say that God "loves all people, regardless of their faults."[4]

A number of psychologists and sociologists have conducted experiments and surveys using different concepts of God. Of particular interest are those that use the Nurturant and Authoritative cognitive models or something similar. Chapter 2 gave evidence that Nurturing parenting produces children who have greater degrees of self-reliance, prosocial behavior, and confidence in social settings, motivation to achieve, and cheerfulness than any other approach to parenting. Research also shows that a Nurturing deity produces more accepting and forgiving people who have better mental health than those who affirm the Authoritative God.[5]

2. Froese and Bader, *America's Four Gods*.

3. For a helpful summary, see the Pew Research Center, "When Americans say."

4. From the Pew study in the preceding note.

5. For an overview of the research, see Johnson et al., "Mind of the Lord."

Researchers typically use an array of adjectives to find out what people believe about God. Those who believe in the Nurturing God describe God as forgiving, gracious, loving, accepting, not controlling, helping, caring, compassionate, generous, merciful, and tolerant. Those who affirm the Authoritative God say God is critical, punishing, judging, stern, wrathful, damning, disapproving, controlling, rigid, strict, and unforgiving. Researchers have discovered that different concepts of God are very important due to a strong association between specific characteristics that religious believers ascribe to God and the values they prioritize in their lives.[6] Researches note that one's view of God is a key predictor of what people believe about issues ranging from health care to guns. The kind of God we believe in more accurately predicts what we value than our denominational affiliation or church attendance.[7] Images of God undergird our ethics and doctrines because they reflect values important to us. These values guide our behavior and govern what we think is right and wrong. Different Gods have different values and those who believe in a particular God tend to share the same values.

RELATIONSHIPS AND MENTAL HEALTH

A number of studies demonstrate strong associations linking a person's view of God to various aspects of life including mental health.[8] For instance, those who believe God is Nurturing are more open to changes in the social order, such as women in leadership roles. A number of positive benefits of belief in a Benevolent God are the following. People exhibit higher degrees of prosocial behavior such as volunteering to help others. They are more cooperative, agreeable, and have better social relationships. They show greater concern for distributive justice—the goods and services of a community should benefit everyone in society. They are more willing to help people outside their tribe—those who are religiously or ethnically different from themselves.[9] Those who believe that God loves them have significantly higher levels of conviction that their life has meaning and

6. Pepper et al., "Multidimensional Religion."

7. Bader and Froese, "Images" and "Unraveling."

8. See Johnson et al., "Mind of the Lord"; Johnson et al., "Friends in High Places"; Wiegand and Weiss, "Affective Reactions"; Flannelly et al., "Beliefs about God"; Simpson et al., "Understanding"; Brokaw and Edwards, "Relationship"; and Levin, "Is Depressed?"

9. Shen et al., "Testing."

purpose.[10] Those who feel secure in God's love have greater life satisfaction and have less loneliness. In addition, they are more humble and less dogmatic.[11] Those with a Nurturing God have more positive views of significant others in their lives and have more secure and trusting attachments to family and teachers.[12] In terms of mental health, those with a Benevolent God have higher self-esteem along with significantly less depression, general anxiety, and obsessive-compulsion.[13] Those who collaborate with God to solve problems show greater sense of personal control in their lives.[14] They have positive coping strategies for traumatic life events.[15] Believers in a forgiving God are more willing to forgive people unconditionally without requiring acts of contrition.[16]

Believers in the Authoritative God exhibit several beneficial characteristics. They have good cooperation with members of their in-group, are more optimistic about the future, and are less likely to cheat.[17] Something that can be either good or bad, depending on the situation, is that they resist changes to the social order because they prefer tradition and conformity. On the negative side, they tend to be highly suspicious of others and are more aggressive.[18] They have less concern for outsiders particularly if they are religiously or ethnically different. They are less tolerant of those who are not like them. Those who are more fearful of God have less humility and hold their beliefs more rigidly. The quality of relationships with significant others is not as strong and they have lower degrees of attachment. They often wait for God to solve problems for them so they feel less in control and they have poorer problem-solving skills. Regarding mental health, they have lower self-esteem, more depression and general anxiety.[19] Those who believe God is judgmental exhibit significantly more social anxiety,

---

10. Stroope et al., "Images."

11. Jankowski and Sandage, "Attachment."

12. Kirkpatrick, "God"; and Kirkpatrick and Shaver, "An Attachment-Theoretical."

13. Benson and Spilka, "God Image"; Buri and Mueller, "Psychoanalytic Theory"; Francis, "God Images"; Bradshaw, et al., "Attachment"; and Bradshaw et al., "Prayer."

14. Pargament et. al., "Religion."

15. Pargament et al., "God help."

16. Krause and Ellison, "Forgiveness."

17. Sethi and Seligman, "Optimism"; Shariff and Norenzayan, "Mean Gods."

18. Johnson et al., "Friends" and Bushman et al., "When God."

19. In addition to the studies mentioned in note 11, see McConnell et al., "Examining."

paranoia, and compulsions.[20] Fear of hell connects to a judgmental deity. Those who fear hell show increased anxiety, sense little control over their lives, and experience higher levels of stress when a loved one dies.[21] Just as their God requires people to perform acts of contrition in order to "deserve" forgiveness, so do they. This behavior is associated with greater depression and lower life satisfaction.

One recent study focused on Calvinism, a particular version of the Authoritative God. The researchers found that those who believe in the Calvinist deity who tightly controls everything that happens and who affirm "gender complementarianism" (women are to be submissive to male authority) are more accepting of domestic violence and suppress its disclosure.[22] They are also intolerant of other Christian views and their religious life is externally regulated and rule-based.[23] These traits align with Authoritative values.

The Faith Matters Survey has an intriguing finding. Researchers asked people how often they felt God's love and/or judgment in their lives. It also inquired about their degree of trust in other people. It turns out that Americans who experience God as loving have far more trust in other people while those who believe they have experienced God's judgment are quite distrusting.[24] Experiencing God as Nurturant cultivates social trust and courtesy while experiencing God as Authoritative fosters stern judgment and lack of civility.

Believers in different Gods also have different views about whether one's economic situation is due to obeying God or not. Both rich and poor Americans tend to believe God is concerned about their personal well-being, but those with lower incomes are far more likely to believe that being poor is God's judgment on them for their moral failures.[25] They believe in the Authoritative God who is angry at their sins so God punishes them by making them poor. Conversely, they think being wealthy is a sign of divine blessing for following God's rules.

Authoritatives believe that fear of punishment is necessary so that people follow the rules. Fear maintains order in society. Nurturants, on the

20. Baylor Religion Survey, "Values and Beliefs," 14.
21. Baylor Religion Survey, "American Values."
22. Jankowki et al., "Religious Beliefs."
23. See the study in note 18 and Sandage et al., "Calvinism."
24. Putnam and Campbell, *American Grace*, 468–71.
25. Froese and Bader, *America's Four Gods*, 114–15.

other hand, believe that love empowers others to do what is right. First John says "God is love" (4:16) and that fear-based religion is contrary to who God is. John writes: "There is no fear in love, but perfect love casts out fear; for fear has to do with punishment, and whoever fears has not reached perfection in love" (4:18). In short, John says that Authoritative religion does not imitate the God of Jesus.

In so many ways, the God we follow makes a huge difference. Just as the Nurturant parenting style produces better quality children, so the Benevolent God produces people who experience better spiritual and mental health. Believers in a Nurturing God exhibit more of the virtues that Jesus and God have so they have better social relationships and greater overall mental health. The evidence from the research supports that believing in the Nurturing God is far more beneficial.

Not only do believers in these two Gods live differently, they even disagree about what God looks like. Facial characteristics are commonly associated with particular types of people so researchers investigated what people think a typical person on welfare or an atheist "looks like." In the experiments, people see a series of pictures of generic faces and they select which one they believe best fits the category. The pictures include traits such as masculine/feminine, dull/bright eyes, and skin tones. Americans think that the typical "atheist" face has small eyes and a narrow chin to indicate their supposed lack of honesty. Even though Christian tradition holds that God does not have a body, artists such as Michelangelo have depicted God with specific facial features. Researchers asked Americans what God looks like.[26] They found that political conservatives see God as older, white, more masculine, powerful, and strict. Political progressives visualize God as younger, less white, less masculine, more loving, and having a slight smile.[27]

WHAT ABOUT GOD THE FATHER?

The Bible often refers to God as "he" and frequently uses the metaphors of king and father for God. Though biblical writers use several female metaphors to understand God, such as a woman giving birth (Isa 42:14, 49:15) or nursing her children (Isa 49:15, 66:12–13), the more common

26. Jackson et al., "Faces of God."

27. The films *Bruce Almighty* and *The Shack* also depict God in less white, less masculine, and more loving terms.

metaphors use ancient male roles. This made sense because, *in their cultural context*, only males had the power to change a person's status or situation in life.[28] Males decided whether to adopt someone into a family or whether to grant someone citizenship. Therefore, it made sense in their ancient culture to talk about how God could change your situation by using metaphors about kings and fathers. In our culture, females have the power to change one's status so the content we give to the metaphors of God as father and mother are different for us than for ancient Israel. In Christian tradition, God is actually neither male nor female since God does not have a physical body. Yet Christian prayers, songs, and liturgy have traditionally spoken of God using masculine pronouns and metaphors. Though many who believe in the Authoritative God say that God has no gender, they do believe that the best way to depict God is through masculine imagery. In addition, some believers in an Authoritative God think that God is a literal male. Thinking of God as male supports their belief that fathers are in charge of the home and only males should hold positions of authority in churches and the work place.

A well-known evangelical theologian once scorned what I had written about God by saying, "Your view of God has feminine characteristics." I was dumbfounded. I could not understand why that was something negative. It finally dawned on me that he considered a God who is open to us and forgives as characteristically feminine. What is wrong with that, I wondered. Do we really want a deity with infinite testosterone? He thought it was inappropriate to depict God with what he considered feminine characteristics. According to Authoritative values, showing mercy and listening to others produces weak people in a dangerous world. Evangelical leader John MacArthur made this point in a 2019 sermon. He said that women typically have compassion, mercy, and kindness that make them "vulnerable." That is why they need males to "protect them from deception."[29] These Authoritatives believe that "women's traits" are negative and since males have more favorable traits, God has male characteristics—stern and strict with low levels of compassion and mercy. That is why males should be in charge of religion, government, and the home.

However, according to the Nurturant way of life, forgiveness and empathy are true virtues because God has them. Such traits are neither feminine nor masculine. Jesus was male and he accepted, forgave, and

28. Sanders, *Theology*, 223–26.
29. MacArthur, "Does the Bible?"

listened to others. Of course, many males have these qualities so these are not distinctly feminine traits. The real problem is that such theologians conceptualize God as a Strict Father whose love is conditional upon obedience and is tough on the kids to make them strong. As a result, they mistakenly believe features such as mercy and openness to others are "feminine" characteristics.

Believers in the Authoritative God belittle the Benevolent God for being a "user-friendly" God. They say it fails to take sin, defined as disobedience to the rules, seriously, and does not give due respect to the divine glory and sovereignty. The Strict Father understanding of God finds it repugnant to think of God cooperating with creatures and not demanding respect and obedience before accepting others. The Nurturant approach is foolishness to Authoritatives because they see it as coddling people, giving things to those who do not deserve it, and fostering disrespect for authority.

Before we leave the subject of God as father, it is instructive to note that Mormons have one of the most thoroughgoing Authoritative father religions in the world. They believe that God is literally, not metaphorically, our father. God and his wife had sex and gave birth to us as spirit beings in the heavenly realm where we existed before our spirit became a human being through our earthly parents. The female deity has no name and has no role other than giving birth to spirit babies. Some feminist Mormons tried to get a conversation about her going in Mormonism but the Mormon male leadership excommunicated them. Leadership in Mormonism is strongly patriarchal, following their God's example. All the authority positions, from the president and twelve apostles to ward leaders are males. The male church leaders get their directions straight from the divine father. Questioning what God ordains is dangerous because it undermines the Mormon way of life. Obedience to the leaders is strictly enforced and those who challenge the rules quickly find themselves silenced or excommunicated. I personally know several Mormons promoting a more Nurturing God. Yet, the entire Mormon culture of salvation depends upon obedience to the practices proscribed by the males.

CONCLUSION

The Nurturant and Authoritative Gods exemplify fundamentally different core values. The different Gods work to create us in their image—and they look very different. What we believe God is like serves as a prototype for our lives—the example for how we should live. The previous two chapters showed that Jesus and many biblical authors taught the Benevolent God and rejected the Authoritative God. This chapter showed that thinking of God as fundamentally loving, forgiving, and open to our prayers fosters values that result in better relationships and mental health. The prophets of the Old Testament rejected false gods that served to support regimes that took advantage of widows and orphans for economic gain. The wealthy thought they had earned God's blessing and the poor deserved to be poor. Today, we need a changing of the Gods. It is time for Christians to reject the false Authoritative deity and worship the true Nurturing God.

5

GRACE AND WHY SOME JUST DON'T GET IT

The philosophy club at a state university sponsored a public forum on "Does God Exist?" The leaders of the club invited me and another professor to serve as resource persons. The atheists and those who believed in God presented reasons for their views with passion. After many exchanges Saul, the president of the philosophy club, said that belief in God was unreasonable and led to immoral positions. At that point, I asked, "Which God don't you believe in? After all, there are many understandings of God." His response was immediate: "The God who damns to hell everyone who never hears of Jesus." "Who believes that?" I asked. He replied, "Christians do." "All Christians?" I asked. "The Christians on this campus do!" was his emphatic reply. I then pointed out that esteemed Christians such as Gregory of Nyssa, Thomas Aquinas, John Wesley, and C. S. Lewis rejected the view that God damns to hell those who've never heard the gospel. After the meeting, Saul talked with me for a long time. At the end he said, "Perhaps I've written off God too soon."

I used to wonder why the same people blasted each book I wrote. It did not matter what the topic was, they threw scathing remarks my way. I now realize that I produced Nurturing theology while they defended Authoritative theology. Our core values were in opposition, resulting in very different ethics and doctrines. The distinctive values of the Nurturing way of life resonate with some understandings of sin, grace, atonement, and hell. Authoritative values are compatible with different views on these topics. This chapter explores these debates.

SIN AND GRACE

For the Nurturant view, the Christian life is primarily about a loving relationship with God and then replicating that love with others. Sin is about relationships: humans are out of proper relationship with God and others. To correct this problem, God welcomes and showers people with hospitality they do not deserve. God seeks to win us back. The New Testament uses a host of metaphors to understand sin and salvation.[1] Here are but a few. Sin is a slave master and salvation is liberation from slavery (Rom 6:6; Heb 2:14–15). Sin is breaking off friendship with God and salvation is reestablishing the friendship (James 4:4). Sin is a sickness that God, the physician, heals (Mark 2:16–17). Sin is being an alien and salvation is God granting you citizenship (Col 1:13). Sinners belong to God for they are God's sheep, coins, and children. They are lost so God goes searching to get them back (Luke 15).

Each metaphor for salvation has a different logic. Someone captured by a slave master is powerless to change their situation. They must wait for someone to pay the ransom for them. If we are lost sheep or lost coins then we must wait for someone to find us. However, if we construe our situation as a disrupted friendship, then we can take action to be reconciled. Even if the offended friend approaches us first, we still have to take some action to amend the relationship. If we are sick and need healing, then we need to follow the prescription from the divine physician. In chapter 2, we saw that there are many ways in English to understand what love is. We think of love as a nutrient ("Her love sustains him"), as fire ("She is burning with devotion"), as magnetism ("They are strongly attracted to each other"), and as traveling together ("Our relationship has come a long way"). Each metaphor has its own set of inferences about what we should do, which is why thinking of love as a journey together means that each person has responsibilities for the relationship while thinking of love as a powerful force ("He was swept off his feet") means that the person is not responsible. So which metaphor for love is the correct one? Which metaphor for salvation is the correct one? Is it liberation from bondage, healing from illness, the granting of citizenship, or lost and found? The wonderful thing is that no single metaphor says everything we want to say about love or salvation. Our experiences of love and salvation are so multifaceted and rich that we need multiple ways to understand them. That is why biblical writers use dozens

---

1. See Sanders, *Theology*, 176–190 and Colijn, *Images of Salvation*.

of metaphors for salvation. Unfortunately, Christians have tried to pick the one metaphor to, like Tolkien's ring, rule them all. That actually discards the many delightful ways of understanding salvation. The truth is that no single metaphor or theory encompasses the wonderfully rich experience of salvation any more than one metaphor captures all the ways of thinking about love. Nurturant Christians should value a constrained pluralism of metaphors for salvation.

The way Authoritatives understand sin and salvation is quite different. Here, sin is primarily the breaking of God's rules. Each person is individually responsible to follow the moral code. Those who transgress receive punishment in order to develop moral strength. It is necessary to treat sin harshly since it rejects divine authority and insults God's holiness. Sin disrespects the honor due God, the highest authority, so it must be punished severely. Salvation occurs when Jesus takes the punishment due us. God grants acceptance to those who acknowledge Jesus as the substitute punished for their sins. Hereafter, believers are to show proper respect to God's authority and obey the moral order.

COMPARISONS

Authoritative theology tells sinners they can become a child of God *if* they believe Jesus saves them from the punishment they deserve. A Nurturant theology says something quite different. As in the parable of the Prodigal Son, God considers people divine children who are lost. Like the father in the parable, God embraces problem children, empowering them to live anew. God invites them to share a meal together and be reconciled. Some Authoritatives say that Jesus' death reconciled God the Father to humans. However, the vast majority of Christian thinkers have said that it is humans who need to be reconciled to God, never that God needs to be reconciled to us (2 Cor 5:19). God is for us from the get-go. When we turn away from God, we follow idols and develop harmful ways of living. Miroslav Volf notes that to forgive someone means to acknowledge that what the person did was wrong. That is why forgiveness is a special kind of gift—it recognizes a wrong but does not punish.[2] One way to translate Paul's description of love is "it keeps no records of wrongs" (1 Cor 13:5). God does not hold our wrongs against us. When God forgives, the idols that hold us captive lose their power. Their grip on us is broken, freeing us to become those who

2. Volf, *Free of Charge*, 130–70.

treat others the way God treats us. This is what happens in the story *Les Misérables*, when the Bishop shows hospitality and then forgiveness to Jean Valjean. He frees him from living according to an eye for an eye to living in grace. What God wants is reconciliation and changed lives, not a business contract that says if you keep your end of the bargain, you gain admission to planet heaven.

It is common to hear people say, "God cannot look on sin." Authoritatives use this to reinforce God's stern disapproval of us. God cannot stand us. Jonathan Edwards said this clearly in his famous sermon "Sinners in the Hands of Angry God," delivered in 1741.[3] He says that all humans "deserve" to be condemned to hell. "The wrath of God is like great waters that are dammed for the present" and "you are every day treasuring up more wrath." At some point God will release the pent-up wrath, sweeping sinners to hell. What does God think of us? "The God that holds you over the pit of hell, much as one holds a spider, or some loathsome insect over the fire, abhors you." He goes on to say that God "will not only hate you, but he will have you, in the utmost contempt." Jesus and the angels, he says, look upon those in hell with satisfaction. The humans in heaven shall "look on the awful spectacle, that they may see what the wrath and fierceness of the Almighty is; and when they have seen it, they will fall down and adore that great power and majesty." Edwards accurately summarizes the way Authoritatives believe God relates to us. Nurturants find this depiction of God lacking in empathy and devoid of love. They can imagine fearing such a deity but not "adoring" it as Edwards does. This understanding of the divine is light years away from the Jesus who forgave those who killed him and said to love those who hate us. The Authoritative God of Edwards hates and detests humans and so is not like Jesus.

Some biblical writers do say that God manifests wrath at some things. Authoritatives interpret this to mean that God carries out wrath on Jesus on the cross or upon humans in hell. This fits with the penal substitutionary view of the atonement (discussed shortly). However, as N. T. Wright shows, according to the book of Romans, God does not direct wrath upon Jesus on the cross or against humans at all.[4] Rather, God is wrathful at Sin, personified as an agent, who has captured us and holds us in bondage to false gods. God condemned Sin for taking us prisoner (Rom 8:3). God did

3. Edwards, "Sinners," 150–67.
4. Wright, *Day the Revolution*, 272–315.

not condemn Jesus as the penal substitution view claims. Rather, God is wrathful at what Sin has done.

Another comparison is that Nurturing theology believes God wants to redeem all humanity and even all creation (Rom 8:22). All are God's children and God wants them back—they are not loathsome insects as Edwards said. God gives everyone an opportunity to fulfill their potential. Authoritatives, on the other hand, believe that God is not interested in outsiders. God's exclusive in-group are the few who follow the divinely established rules pertaining to salvation. It is immoral for God to throw seeds of grace around indiscriminately, as in the parable of the Sower. Instead, God should give the grace seeds to those who will responsibly cultivate the seeds. Calvinists take this a step further and say that God was never interested in saving everyone. God eternally selected a few people to save so Jesus' atonement is only for those few.

Nurturants believe God includes all in grace but does not force us to receive it and return home. As a result, some exclude themselves from God's love. Jesus told a parable about a king who sent out messengers to invite the nobility to the wedding of his son (Matt 22). However, they refuse to attend. The king is determined to have a hall filled with guests for the wedding so he tells the messengers to invite everyone they meet on the streets. And they came, filling the hall. Jesus told this parable in response to the religious leaders who rejected him as the messiah. In the story, the king invites everyone to the party but there are some party-poopers who refuse grace.

Indiscriminate forgiveness and inclusion of all are incompatible with Authoritative values. Authoritatives think this is an unrealistic approach to life. It damages the moral order. People should not get something for nothing. Free riders will take advantage of us. Jesus says to forgive people seventy-seven times (Matt 18:22), but Authoritatives say that approach will only encourage people to sin. In order to teach people to live responsibly we need to punish lawbreakers severely. Some years ago, the youth leaders at a church called a meeting of the parents. The leaders had given a questionnaire about Christian doctrines to the youth group and then followed up with some interviews. They said that on one level, the youth talked about grace and forgiveness, but the leaders were concerned that these ideas were not what they actually believed. I thought this made sense because though church leaders "preached" grace what they did was different. If someone messed up, they were rejected. Time after time, those in the church who did something that the leaders did not approve received rebukes. Often, such folks had to leave the congregation. Leaders did not practice forgiveness and reconciliation and the youth clearly got the message.

ATONEMENT

From the fourth through eighth centuries, major church councils debated an array of topics but no council ever convened to resolve how Jesus' work of salvation (atonement) should be understood. The New Testament writers used a wide array of metaphors to construe what Jesus has accomplished—from the liberation of slaves to adoption. Over the centuries, Christians developed several views of atonement and some of these resonate with Nurturing values while other models make more sense in an Authoritative framework.

In *The Day the Revolution Began*, acclaimed New Testament scholar, N. T. Wright does a wonderful job of showing that the New Testament writers understood the atonement of Jesus in Nurturing rather than Authoritative terms. The cross of Jesus is, he says, about God's incredible love for humans who are in bondage to idols. Jesus frees us from the grip of the false gods so that we may live out our original vocation of being the likeness of God in the world. God was not angry with us and God did not hold our sins against us. Rather, as Paul declares, in divine forbearance God "passed over" our sins (Rom 3:25). Wright points out that there is nothing about God punishing anyone in this context. God deals with the human problem but it has nothing to do with moral accounting and punishment. Paul says that Jesus' death showed that God loves the weak, ungodly, enemies, and sinners (Rom 5:6–10). The cross did not change God's attitude towards us because God always loved us. It confirmed God's everlasting love of humans, blemishes and all. The cross demonstrates that nothing can separate us from God's love, not our idolatry nor our leaving home to become a prodigal (Rom 8:38–39). God forgives and says, "Let's try again." Wright says forgiveness is the power of God's revolution for it makes possible a new way of life. God does not hold the past against us and this allows a new era to begin. Like the father of the prodigal son, God welcomes the "lost" and "dead" children back with a warm embrace. God restores us to our true home and calling. The power of love liberates us to live a Nurturing life.

Several "theories" of atonement are compatible with Nurturant values. For example, the *Christus Victor* theory was extremely popular in the first several centuries of the church and remains common in the Eastern

Orthodox Church. Recently, it has made a comeback among Protestants. According to this model, evil forces have taken humans captive but Jesus' death and resurrection were victorious over these powers and set us free to return home to God. C. S. Lewis's *The Lion, The Witch, and the Wardrobe* uses this idea when Aslan gives his life to defeat the Witch's hold on Edmund as well as to liberate all the creatures the witch has turned to stone. Another view comes from Abelard in the twelfth century. He said Jesus' atonement is primarily about demonstrating God's amazing love. This "model of love" theory says that Jesus' life and death exemplified the way God relates to us. Divine hospitality empowers us to love as Jesus did. Another approach is the "scapegoat" view, which says that when a society faces severe hardships it will scapegoat individuals or minorities by blaming them for the misfortunes. The community drives the scapegoats away or punishes them in violent ways. In his life and on the cross, Jesus unmasks this pattern of scapegoating and frees us from blaming others and mistreating them for our problems. Any Nurturing approach to atonement will hold divine love and forgiveness as central. In addition, it will emphasize that atonement results in an ongoing transformation of how people relate to one another. Just as no single metaphor says everything we want to say about salvation, neither does any single theory of atonement. Nurturants can welcome a number of views (see chapter 8).

Because Authoritative values are extremely different from Nurturing values, they construct radically different views of atonement. In particular, their values direct them to see the death of Jesus as payment and punishment for sins. In the Authoritative way of life there is no free lunch and God does not allow free riders. Contrary to 1 Corinthians 13:5, which says that love "keeps no record of wrongs," the Authoritative God keeps meticulous records of human good and bad deeds in the divine moral accounting books (see chapter 3). Moral accounting means that when someone does something good to you then you "owe" them an equal good in return. When someone harms you then you owe them an equal harm in retribution. According to Authoritative theology, this is exactly how God operates. When people disobey God, then God must exact a payment equal to the sin. Unfortunately, human sin runs up debts we cannot pay. Why does not God simply forgive us? That is what the Nurturing God does. The answer, as Anselm in the eleventh century said, is that it is not "fitting" for God to forgive us.[5] Why? Because it is wrong for God to show mercy without

5. Anselm, *Why God*, book 1, chapter 12.

any payment. Somebody must pay for sin. In other words, according to the moral accounting system, it is immoral for God to forgive people—it leaves the books unbalanced.

In Authoritative theology, there are two main views of how Jesus pays for sins. The first view is the satisfaction theory developed by Anselm. He used the medieval feudal system to explain it. When those under the authority of the king disobeyed the king, they brought dishonor on the king. To restore the honor, the king demanded satisfaction (payment). The higher the king the greater the dishonor. The greater the dishonor the larger the payment required. Since God is infinitely above all human kings, human sin incurs an infinite debt to God's honor. Humans cannot pay an infinite debt so we all deserve hell. Fortunately, Jesus lived a life of perfect obedience to God's laws and, because Jesus is also God, he made an infinite payment to restore God's honor. God received payment in full and so was "satisfied."

The Mormon view of atonement also centers on Jesus' perfect obedience that pleases God the father. Jesus, in Mormon theology, is the very first spirit being born to Mr. and Mrs. God. He is literally our eldest brother who, like the older brother in the parable of the Prodigal Son, always obeys the father. For Mormons, the atonement took place in the garden of Gethsemane when Jesus said three times that he would do the father's will. Jesus' submission to the father's commands is the example for all Mormons to imitate by obeying the instructions of their leaders. Though there are some Mormon thinkers who suggest other views of atonement, the dominant view fits with the strong Authoritative values in their religion.

The second way that Jesus "pays" for our sins is the penal substitution view. It is the primary theory of atonement in Roman Catholic and Protestant churches—a triumph of Authoritative ingenuity. Like the satisfaction theory, it uses the metaphor of moral accounting in which God keeps record books of sin. God sets out the laws that humans are to obey. God cannot allow sin to go unpunished because this would encourage disrespect for authority and undermine the social order. If God simply forgives, then God is an unjust ruler. The righteous judge finds us guilty and sentences us to the penalty we deserve—death and hell. However, instead of punishing us, God punishes Jesus in our place. Jesus lived a life of perfect obedience to God's laws and so did not deserve punishment. By dying as our substitute, Jesus paid God for our sins and balanced the moral books.

There are a number of things wrong with the Authoritative views of atonement. To begin, they think that Jesus was wrong to tell the parable of the Prodigal Son as he did. They say the father in the parable should punish the son or make him pay up in order balance the moral books. They affirm the reciprocity principle that if someone does harm to you, then you should do them an equivalent harm in return—an eye for an eye. God returns harm for harm, just not on us. Jesus is the one who receives God's harm (punishment) in our place. However, Jesus, Paul, and Peter explicitly reject the moral teaching of repaying evil for evil and tell us to do good to those who harm us (Matt 5:38–41; 1 Thess 5:15; 1 Pet 3:9). According to the Authoritative models of atonement, God behaves exactly how Jesus, Paul, and Peter said not to.

It is important to note that God does *not forgive* anyone in the satisfaction or penal substitution theories. No, God places the full penalty on Jesus—somebody must pay. If somebody else pays my debt in full, then it is wrong to say my debt was forgiven. Forgiveness means cancellation of the debt, not that someone else paid it. If I do something to deserve punishment but one of my siblings is punished in my place, then I am not forgiven. Rather, the penalty was carried out—just not on me. In both the satisfaction and penal views, God the father exacts the retribution due us by inflicting it on God the son. Jesus is the substitute who pays for us. God punished Jesus in our place. Even though those who affirm the penal substitution view like to say that God forgives, that is quite mistaken. What occurs here is *vicarious punishment,* not forgiveness!

People are so used to hearing that penal substitution is how God forgives that they have a hard time seeing that it is not forgiveness at all. Perhaps some examples will help. If you have a loan from a bank there are two ways the debt can be cancelled without you paying it off. The first is when someone else pays the loan on your behalf. In this case, bank does not say, "your loan is forgiven." Rather, it says, "it is paid in full." On the other hand, the bank could simply "forgive" the loan without anyone paying for it. Nations sometimes forgive the loans of other nations. This is what the New Testament says God does—God forgives and does not require payment from anyone. In a Nurturant approach, God simply cancels the debt. The death of Jesus is not for God's benefit. Jesus does not "pay the price" demanded by God to settle the divine accounting books. Instead, the death of Jesus is for our benefit. It reconciles us to God, demonstrating the power of forgiveness.

N. T. Wright refers to the popular understanding of the penal substitution view as a "paganized soteriology" (means of salvation), which says God needs to be appeased by punishing Jesus. God is a vengeful, bloodthirsty deity who tortures Jesus in order to be satisfied. The angry God who hates sinners and kills Jesus does not sound like good news or love. Though Authoritatives attempt to say that the deity who demands obedience as a condition of acceptance is practicing love, it is actually a perverted understanding of love (see chapter 3). As Wright observes, it twists the gospel story of genuine love and forgiveness into one in which an angry God, upset about rule breaking, punishes Jesus and then punishes everyone to hell who fails to believe in Jesus' substitutionary punishment. This is the "Authoritative gospel," but it is not the gospel of Jesus. The God who says, "If you don't love me exactly as I stipulate, then I will torture you forever," is not the God of Jesus. If one begins with the idea that God demands keeping divine laws in order to be accepted, then the cross as forgiveness, which sets us free to follow our divine vocation, makes no sense at all. That is why Authoritative values twist the Jesus story to fit into their moral accounting mold so that somebody pays the punishment God demands. Defenders of the penal substitution theory tend to think that any criticism of it is an attack on the gospel itself. The reason why this seems obvious to them is that penal substitution fits hand-in-glove with Authoritative values. However, the "Authoritative gospel" is, as Wright very carefully shows, not what the New Testament teaches.

One reason that the satisfaction and penal substitution theories became widely accepted in the Western church is that they are built upon the moral accounting system that became pervasive in the Middle Ages. During this time the religious system of "penance" developed. The idea is that one needed to perform actions such as reciting prayers or building an orphanage to *pay* for one's sins. The doctrine of purgatory also made use of moral accounting. Those who died with sins they had not done penance for had to suffer in purgatory after death before they could enter heaven. God is a strict judge who ensures payment for every sin, in this life or in purgatory, until the moral books are balanced. The Protestant Reformers rejected the notion of purgatory but they used the moral accounting view to argue that Jesus paid for our sins. That is why penal substitution made sense to them. Fortunately, there were voices, even in the Middle Ages, who rejected the God who demands punishment for rule breakers. Julian of Norwich, for instance, presented an alternative when she said that God is our "very loving mother and father" who forgives without exacting punishment and who embraces us even when we fail. Nurturing Christians, such as Julian, have spoken for the true God against those who filter the gospel through Authoritative values.

Others criticize the penal theory because Christians have used it to justify slaughtering Jews and even other Christians in the name of the cross. If God hates and tortures those outside the tribe, then so can we. Penal substitution has even justified telling women suffering from spousal abuse that it is "your cross to bear." A recent study shows that people who believe in penal substitution show significantly less concern to reduce pain and suffering in people's lives.[6] This theology leads us away from human flourishing.

A Nurturant theology of atonement sees it as forgiveness, reconciliation, and restorative justice whereas an Authoritative approach understands it as punishment, demanding payment, and retributive justice. One side sees it as primarily about relationships while the other sees it as a contractual or legal affair. Penal substitution and satisfaction views of atonement may result in folks being thankful for escaping punishment, but they do not result in forgiveness. Nor do these views entail the transformation of how people live. For many Authoritative Christians, the only thing important about Jesus is the day he died on the cross to pay for their sins. Salvation is primarily a transaction Jesus made to pay our account to God. The life of Jesus is downplayed because there is nothing here about following the example of Jesus. A Nurturant view of salvation holds that Jesus' life is an exemplar for Christians to follow in his steps. It leads to an ongoing relationship with God and the transformation of Christian communities who practice atonement—understood as forgiveness and reconciliation—in the way they relate to others.[7]

EUCHARIST AND BAPTISM

The Benevolent God works in Nurturing ways so we need to frame the Christian practices of baptism and communion in these same values. The four Gospels say the death of Jesus occurred during the feast of Passover. Jesus modified the Passover service into what became the Christian practice of the Lord's Supper/Eucharist. The Passover service is about the liberation of Israel from bondage. During the celebration, people ate lamb to identify

6. Hydinger et al., "Penal."

7. McKnight holds that Christians should practice atonement to others: *Community*.

themselves with God's salvation. They did not kill the lamb as punishment for sins. This is important so that we properly understand the meaning of communion. Jesus tells his disciples that the bread and wine at the meal are his body and blood and that by eating it they identify with the liberation from evil achieved by Jesus' death and resurrection. The Gospels frame the death of Jesus in terms of Passover and liberating people from oppression, not as God punishing Jesus. In light of this, the communion service is a fellowship meal (a supper) in God's home to celebrate our liberation (1 Cor 10–11). It is not about Jesus suffering the punishment due us by a deity who requires retribution. Thinking of the Lord's Supper as penalty for a legal infraction misses that it is really about God's incredible welcome to the divine banquet. In the early centuries, Christians thought the Eucharist was about new ways of life brought about by the powerful love of Jesus that produced a new exodus into God's country. However, after the seventh century, once the Authoritative use of divine moral accounting became influential the Eucharist was about Jesus paying the price for our rule breaking.

Just as the Exodus brought Israel from Egypt to God, so Jesus frees us from bondage and brings us to God. God has already liberated us, now God invites us to participate in an ongoing relationship with God. After God brought the Israelites out of Egypt, God told Israel "I bore you on eagles' wings and brought you to myself" (Exod 19:4). Jesus' death and resurrection bear us to God's home where we live by a new name. Living in God's estate empowers us to live according to God's values. In baptism, Christians wash away the past life in order to live anew. Upon leaving the baptismal waters Christians are to "clothe themselves in Christ" (Gal 3:27). Yes, Jesus founded a brand of apparel! By wearing Jesus' brand of clothing, we identify with him and begin to resemble him. Communities of believers practice the way of Jesus in their daily lives. Salvation is not merely something God does for us. It is also something we do with God to redeem our communities.

ATTITUDES TOWARDS NON-CHRISTIANS

What about non-Christians who have not heard the gospel of Jesus in a sufficient way? People may have heard about Jesus but in a way that does not communicate what the gospel is really about. Most of these people grow up in a religion other than Christianity. Historically, Christians have held that Jesus is the only one who brings salvation. Most have also said that God wants to redeem every single human. If so, does God make the salvation in Jesus available to everyone? A 2007 survey asked Americans whether non-Christians can go to heaven.[8] Overwhelmingly, Americans believe this is the case with the breakdown as follows: Catholics 83 percent, Mainline Protestants 79 percent, Black Protestants 62 percent, and evangelicals 54 percent.

Throughout history, Christians have held at least eight different views about the salvation of non-Christians.[9] Three of the most popular views are restrictivism, postmortem evangelization, and inclusivism. Restrictivism says that the only ones saved are those who learn about Jesus and accept Jesus' payment for your sins before they die. The possibility of salvation is limited to those who become Christians in this life. This view is widely held by Authoritative evangelicals. They believe that God set out the moral rules to live by but all humans have disobeyed God and so deserve hell. God has provided a way of escape from this punishment and it is limited to those in this life who accept that Jesus died for them. There is no opportunity after death and no other way to find salvation. The boats containing humanity have all sunk and now humans desperately tread water in the ocean. In response, God sends Jesus to captain the lifeboat of salvation. The lifeboat never makes it to everyone but some are fortunate that it reaches them and they climb aboard. The rest will drown in hell. God accepts those who make it into the life boats (the church) but not the others. Some might say this is unjust since the lifeboat does not reach everyone and give them an opportunity for deliverance. However, the restrictivist replies that the playing field is level since everyone had an opportunity not to sin. If they had not broken God's laws, their boats would not have sunk. Just as Authoritatives say that people should not blame the educational or criminal justice systems for their problems, so also those who have never heard the gospel should blame themselves, not God's system of salvation. God set up the rules by which the lifeboat operates and there are no exceptions to the rules. They get what they deserve. If someone thinks this system is unfair, the response is "who are you to question God?" Believers in a judgmental God tend to say that only those with this theology will make it to heaven. Since they don't think that people who attend churches with a different theology will be in heaven, they certainly don't believe non-Christians have a chance.[10]

8. Putnam and Campbell, *American Grace*, 534–40.

9. For a discussion of all the views, see my website drjohnsanders.com/religiouspluralism as well as Sanders, *No Other Name* and *What About*.

10. Froese and Bader, "God in America."

A Nurturing theology thinks of justice quite differently. Distributive justice is important so that people have access to the goods and services of society. As much as possible people should have the same opportunities to fulfill their potential in life. Christians who think this way find the restrictivist view morally repugnant. Those with Authoritative values often claim that Nurturants don't believe in justice. They do, but for them justice includes more than just retribution for wrongdoing. Nurturing Christians have developed several views about how God makes the salvation in Jesus accessible. One view is postmortem evangelization. Death cannot prevent God from pursuing the welfare of people so God provides people an opportunity to become a follower of Jesus after death. This view was popular in the early church and many Protestants today hold it. Another view, inclusivism, says that Jesus is the only savior and that God wants to save everyone. It holds that knowledge of Jesus is not necessary for God to grant salvation to someone. The Holy Spirit cannot be controlled or contained within the church. The Spirit works even outside the church to make all persons more Nurturing and Jesus saves those who respond to the Spirit. Jesus saves them in the afterlife even if they do not practice Christianity now. Proponents of this view include luminaries such as Thomas Aquinas, John Wesley, and C. S. Lewis. It is the most widespread view among Catholics and Protestants today.

Authoritative evangelicals like to say that restrictivism is "the" biblical view and that Christians who have differing views are either ignorant or willfully sinful. However, proponents of each of view use biblical texts to support their case. Once again, the watershed divide is between Nurturing and Authoritative values. The two sides have opposing understandings of both love and justice. The postmortem salvation and inclusivism views believe that divine love and justice ensure that the lifeboat reaches everyone. Christians with Nurturant values find that views such as these make more sense to them in light of what they believe God to be like.

HELL

Surveys show that belief in hell has declined among Americans over the past century. In fact, from 2006–2011 belief in hell dropped by 6 percent among people over thirty and by 12 percent in people under thirty.[11] By "hell," Americans typically mean a view called eternal conscious

11. Putnam and Campbell, *American Grace*, 559.

punishment, according to which people in hell are aware of their suffering and it never ends. Proponents of eternal conscious punishment debate whether the flames of hell are literal or figurative and most evangelicals who affirm the view believe the flames are a metaphorical, not literal, way of communicating that those in hell are conscious of their suffering. Most surveys, however, are not aware that Christians historically have held to a spectrum of views about (1) what hell is like, (2) who goes to hell, and (3) whether it lasts forever.[12] Each view supports its case with different biblical texts and theological arguments. Christians who affirm views other than eternal torment hold different views regarding the nature of God and the purpose of divine judgment.

One view says that those who, in the end, refuse God's grace will cease to exist. Hell means the annihilation of the impenitent. Annihilationism (also called conditional immortality) says that God grants immortality to those who accept divine grace. Those who reject grace cease to exist. Because they cease to exist, there is no everlasting suffering. Another view believes that the gates of hell cannot prevent God from entering. When Jesus died, he descended to hell and offered release to those who wanted to leave. The old adage, "You haven't got a preacher's chance in hell," is false. God gives those in hell the opportunity to accept God's forgiveness and enter heaven. At least some do. A third position, universal salvation, takes this a step further saying that hell will eventually be empty. This view goes back to the early church, has always been common in the Eastern Orthodox Church, and a number of evangelicals and Catholics have defended it in recent years.[13] Some proponents are "hopeful" that all will freely return to God but they are not certain this will happen. Others are confident this will occur. Both sides agree that God never gives up and neither time nor hell prevent God from working to achieve the goal of redeeming everyone. God endures the rejection by some of God's children and patiently seeks to win them back, no matter how long it takes. The hope is that God will not have any permanent problem children.

Each of the last three views on hell just discussed believe the eternal conscious torment view is morally repulsive. An everlasting torture chamber or eternal concentration camp is incompatible with God's love and justice. What purpose does punishing people forever accomplish except vindictiveness? There is a meme on the internet that captures what

12. For overviews of each position, see the section on hell at drjohnsanders.com.

13. See Sanders, "Raising Hell" and Baker, *Razing Hell*.

Nurturing Christians think of the eternal torment view. It begins with the famous painting of Jesus outside a home knocking on the door. Jesus says, "Let me in" to which a voice replies, "Why?" Jesus says, "So I can save you." "From what?" asks the person inside the house. "From what I'm going to do to you if you don't let me in," says Jesus.

A Nurturant God loves each person and seeks their highest good. God wants everyone to fulfill their potential. God sees all humans as God's children who are lost or deathly sick and God wants them restored to home and health. God does correct the children and seek to change them. Divine judgment is for the sake of restoring the damaged relationship. Christians with Nurturing values think of God and divine judgment very differently than do Authoritative Christians.

The eternal conscious punishment view fits with Authoritative values. God gave the moral rules and people had a chance to follow the rules but chose not to. God is a by-the-book judge who must punish lawbreakers to maintain the moral order. One could inquire: why does God punish people after death? The answer is that many if not most people are not punished appropriately in this life so it has to be in the next life. All right, but why does it have to be everlasting punishment? The reason is that God is an infinite being so breaking God's laws incurs an infinite penalty, which means that people should be punished infinitely (eternally) in hell. Okay, but why do those in hell have to be conscious of their torment? Because if they are not aware of their suffering then it is not really punishment. Proponents of eternal conscious torment claim that any of the other views of hell have a wimpy deity or fail to take sin seriously. They say those condemned to hell are not God's children but rebels who sought to overthrow God's rule. God rightfully withholds love from them and damns them. When Rob Bell published his book about heaven and hell, *Love Wins*, Authoritative evangelicals hurled vitriol at him on social media and rushed out seven books against it within six months. All seven used the same reasons. Bell does not believe in divine justice or holiness.[14] What went undetected in this brouhaha was that Bell affirms Nurturing views of God, justice, and sin.

When it comes to the topics of the fate of non-Christians and hell, Authoritatives love to quote Jesus' instruction to "Enter through the narrow gate; for the gate is wide and the road is easy that leads to destruction and there are many who take it. For the gate is narrow and the road is hard that leads to life, and there are few who find it" (Matt 7:13–14). They take this to

14. See Sanders, "Raising Hell."

mean that God saves only Christians while everyone else goes to hell. If you do not adhere to the Authoritative way by keeping all the rules, then you go to hell. However, these verses are actually about the Nurturant way of life. Just look at the context. Jesus says to "do to others as you would have them do to you" and then immediately says to "enter through the narrow gate."[15] The "Golden Rule" is the narrow gate! Jesus is saying that loving our enemies, forgiving others, and welcoming the undeserving is the narrow road we should walk. The way of Jesus is not an easy way of life. It took some doing but God finally got the Apostle Peter to understand that "God shows no partiality but in every nation anyone" who lives the way of Nurturant love is welcomed by God (Acts 10:34–35).

CONCLUSION

Nurturant and Authoritative Christians have very different sets of values and different understandings of justice, so it is not surprising they end up with different views on sin, grace, atonement, salvation of non-Christians, and hell. They also have different understandings of what is happening in the ritual of the Eucharist or Lord's Supper. Benevolent Christians believe God is fundamentally loving. God loves us and welcomes us into the divine presence to transform us. God sees humans as lost or sick children who need to be restored. Jesus is the savior who demonstrates God's amazing love and works to reconcile us to God. Spiritual life is primarily about relationships with God and others. The justice of God flows out of the divine love so God seeks ways to make divine grace accessible to all people. The divine love wants all people to have a relationship with God and this includes non-Christians. Everyone is welcomed. God invites all to the wedding party and if there are any party-poopers, it is because they refuse to attend.

An Authoritative theology thinks of sin in contractual terms. God is tough on crime so someone must pay for sin. Jesus satisfies God's vengeance by suffering the punishment due us. The moral books are balanced and the moral order safeguarded. God gives grace only to God's tribal in-group so there is no hope for the salvation of non-Christians. God's rescue boat never reaches the majority of people who have ever lived. God has no compassion on those who drown. They disobeyed the infinite authority so they get what they deserve—God casts them into hell and torments them forever.

15. I owe this insight to Brad Jersak.

Grace is God's fundamental way of relating to us. However, Authoritative types "just don't get it" because grace runs counter to their fundamental values.

6

FOR THE BIBLE TELLS ME SO

The pastor set his Bible on the table, pointed to it and asked me, "Why did you put a question mark where God put a period?" I had recently published a book on the different Christian positions regarding whether Jesus' atonement could save non-Christians. The pastor was upset that my book called into question what he believed was the clear teaching of the Bible, so he called the president of my college to complain and urge him to fire me. The president encouraged him to sit down and talk with me and, to his credit, the pastor did. His opening accusation was abrasive but I checked my desire to fire back at him and asked him which biblical texts he felt supported his view. Over the next hour, I was able to help him see how other Christians interpreted those passages. In addition, I showed him the biblical texts proponents of the other views would ask him to explain. When we parted, he had not changed his mind about which view was correct, but did say that he now realized that what the Bible taught on the subject was not as clear-cut as he had thought. To me, this was a significant realization for an Authoritative to arrive at. We parted on amicable terms while still disagreeing about the topic.

THE NATURE OF THE BIBLE

Christians with a Nurturing orientation find it helpful to think of the Bible as a gift from a person who wants to foster a loving relationship. It is a means of grace that nurtures us to follow the path of God and relate to others as God relates to us. The Bible most clearly presents this guidance in the writings about Jesus because Jesus is the primary exemplar of what God is like. In the Old Testament, the "word" of God was the path to follow. The Gospel of John says *Jesus is the word of God* who reveals what God is like and shows us the path to walk. The purpose of the New Testament is to share with us what Jesus was like and begin to think through what he means for our lives. The New Testament shows how the early Jesus community interpreted and lived out the way of Jesus in their cultural setting. The Holy Spirit uses the stories and commentary on Jesus to guide us on the path of God. The Bible is one of several resources God has provided to assist us in living out the Christian life. The Bible provides an overarching narrative about who God is, the situation we find ourselves in, and what God has done to help us. It is a love story. The overarching message is God's amazing love even though some biblical texts struggle with what God is like.

The Bible provides examples of how to live out the journey of faith. The stories and reflections shape our own spiritual narratives. Hence, the Bible is not an operator's manual or rule book. It is an invitation to a way of life, a pilgrimage, not a list of rules to memorize. There are moral maxims in the Bible, yet they are not ends in themselves but means to help the believing community function together. The moral maxims exist for the sake of relationships. A Nurturing theology respects the Bible and sees it as an instrument the Spirit uses to assist us on our journey. Yet, as we shall see, it does not approach the Bible with an all-or-nothing attitude.

Authoritative theology thinks of the Bible quite differently. The Bible is more of a manual for how to operate moral and doctrinal machinery. It is a rulebook of clear teachings. The teachings are timeless truths independent of ones' cultural context. Nearly 50 percent of Authoritatives believe the Bible has no errors of any kind and most agree that whatever the Bible says about a topic is correct.[1] Proponents of this view tend to say that the Bible is the actual word of God, word for word, and interpret it literally. Around 66 percent of Americans in 1965 agreed that the Bible is the word of God and affirmed reading it literally.[2] By 2008 only 29 percent of Americans held this view and most of them were evangelicals.

One reason that many Authoritatives think we must read the Bible literally is due to a mistaken view of truth.[3] Only literal statements, they claim, are morally and theologically true. Figurative language cannot be true. True

1. Hetherington and Weiler, *Prius*, 34.

2. Putnam and Campbell, *American Grace*, 112.

3. See Sanders, *Theology*, 221–29.

morals and doctrines must be clear and precise. Only literal language can accomplish this, so literal interpretation is the only way to read the Bible. Of course, they admit that the Bible contains figurative language, but they seek to translate any metaphors into literal statements.

The Authoritative understanding of truth and meaning is not in accord with how the human mind operates and how language actually works. Much of what we think is literal is actually not. For instance, take the statements: "I see your point" and "That claim is too much to swallow." These ordinary statements seem literal but they are actually metaphorical. We use metaphors to reason about, to understand, all sorts of topics. The inability to swallow an idea means to think of ideas in terms of food. Of course, ideas are not literally food. Yet, thinking of ideas as food helps us quickly get the meaning. English speakers regularly use vision/seeing metaphorically to mean that we know something. If something is easy or difficult to see, then it is easy or hard to understand. Most of our language in ordinary life is figurative. There is literal language such as "Harry and Susan love each other" and "Tammy helped me pick up the yard after the storm." However, literal language tends to be rudimentary and skeletal. For more robust meaning about love we use figurative language such as "Harry was swept off his feet by Susan" and "our relationship has overcome many obstacles." Experiments show that we typically understand figurative language more quickly than literal language. In addition, figurative language communicates more meaning than bare-bones literal expressions. For instance, the statement, "There is steam coming out his ears" conveys the degree of anger someone has that "He is angry" does not. In terms of how the human mind works, figurative language is the normal and superior way of conveying meaning and truth. Hence, it should not surprise us that most of the Bible is composed of ordinary figurative language.

In addition, Authoritative thinkers strive to achieve a single correct meaning of each biblical passage that all genuine "Bible-believing" Christians agree to. In seminary, I took a course on biblical interpretation. The professor was an acclaimed biblical scholar who taught us detailed procedures for interpreting the Bible that, if followed, would result in everyone agreeing on the meaning of the passage. One day I asked in class, "Do you mean that if we follow your detailed procedures we will arrive at the meaning, the whole meaning, and nothing but the meaning, so help our method of interpretation?" He replied "Yes." I then asked him to explain why he and another professor at the school, who used the same method, disagreed about the interpretation of some important biblical texts. According to his method, both interpreters should agree on the meaning. His witty response was "Oh, John, that's an easy one. Depravity!" The class roared with laughter. I then said, "If that is the case, then you didn't shoot your method in the foot. You shot it in the head. If all of us are depraved, then no supposedly absolute method of interpretation is going to get all Christians to agree."

Chapter 7 discusses the tenacity with which Authoritative believers adhere to the belief that the Bible "clearly teaches" what they believe on any particular topic. I cannot count the number of times people have told me the "clear" biblical teaching about hell, baptism, the Lord's Supper, atonement, and a host of other doctrines. If I disagree with them on any point, then they conclude that I am either stupid or not a genuine Bible-believing Christian. However, the flood of multi-views books in which evangelical scholars debate other evangelical scholars about what the Bible teaches on everything from salvation to evolution ought to make it clear that sincere and responsible Christians have not been able to agree on what the Bible teaches on these topics.[4] Christians throughout history have not been able to agree on the meaning of practices central to the religion such as the Lord's Supper and baptism.

However, this does not mean that Christians believe whatever they want. There are constraints on the possible meanings of texts. Though words typically have a range of meanings, they do not have just any meaning. For example, if someone says, "Jesus is savior" means "Susan has a mole on her left leg," we do not take this interpretation seriously. In addition, there are historical traditions of Christian belief and practice that guide how people read Scripture. We see how others have interpreted and applied biblical ideas in their cultural and historical setting. Traditions are one resource God uses to guide us. What Christians have believed and practiced in the past is helpful, though not foolproof. The church is a pilgrim people and we have not arrived at our destination. Sometimes we disagree with one another about what the Bible means and which direction we should go. We need to learn to discuss our differences over interpretations more civilly. This comes much easier for those with a Nurturing orientation than for Authoritatives. Prototypical Christianity, what most people say is the center of the religion, is comprised of some general beliefs and practices. Beyond these general agreements, there will be diversity of thought and ranges of views. In other words, we should *expect* Christians to agree on a few topics

4. For an insightful critique of this approach, see Smith, *Bible*.

and disagree on a host of topics. That is normal Christianity. A Nurturing way of life recognizes that we can and should take stances on matters of concern to us. Yet, it also inculcates openness towards others and humility in the way we hold our convictions.

USING THE BIBLE TO SET ASIDE BIBLICAL TEACHINGS

Authoritative believers like to preach that believing in the Bible is an "all-or-nothing" affair. If you do not follow all the teachings of the Bible, then you are not following God completely. You are picking and choosing what to believe. One must believe every single teaching in the Bible or you are not a faithful Christian. The rhetoric sounds definitive—no wiggle room, no exceptions. However, they do not actually practice what they preach here (not even fundamentalists). From the time of the apostles to today, Christians have found principled ways to revise or reject biblical teachings they found objectionable. The real debates were about which biblical teachings to adopt, which to adapt, and which to abort.

To begin, it is important to note that biblical writers sometimes revised and set aside other biblical teachings.[5] One example is Exodus 34:5–7, which revises one of the Ten Commandments in Exodus 20. That commandment says that God's love is conditional upon obedience—God will love us only if we obey. However, Exodus 34 makes several changes to this text. It removes the conditional element from the text—God is going to love no matter what. It also changes the word order so that divine love comes first and divine judgment comes last. The book of Exodus revises itself about what God is like.

Though Jesus manifests tremendous continuity with the Old Testament, he does set aside some important scriptural teachings.[6] For example, Jews and Romans commonly used the Old Testament dietary regulations to identify God's in-group, the Jews. However, Jesus said that it is not what goes into a person that makes them impure, but what comes out. Hence, "he declared all foods clean," setting aside all the scriptural laws about food (Mark 7:14–23). Another example is the Sabbath. Numbers forbids even picking up sticks on the Sabbath—they killed a man for doing it (15:32–36).

---

5. For lots of examples of how biblical writers change what other biblical writers said, see Enns, *Incarnation*.

6. Jesus adapted and aborted key beliefs and values of his day. See Wright, *Jesus*, 218–19 and 384–55.

On a couple of occasions, religious Authoritatives confronted Jesus about working on the Sabbath. They caught Jesus harvesting grain on the Sabbath (Mark 2:23–28) and healing people on the Sabbath (John 5 and 9). Some Authoritatives said that Jesus "is not from God, for he does not observe the Sabbath" (John 9:16). Jesus says it is fine to work on the Sabbath because God works on the Sabbath (John 5:17). Another instance is the woman who was bleeding. According to Scripture, anyone she touched rendered them religiously impure, so when she reached out and touched Rabbi Jesus it was a big deal. However, instead of enforcing punishment Jesus praises and blesses her (Luke 8:43–48). Jesus is an example of how to set aside even widely practiced scriptural teachings.

Another example is the contentious debate that occupies many passages of the New Testament. The Old Testament lifts up some Gentiles (non-Jews), such as Zipporah, Jethro, and Naaman as worthy people. Yet, there are also many nasty things said about Gentiles. They are not part of the people of God. At the time of Jesus many believed that God would only accept Gentiles if they converted to Judaism. This was the practice for many centuries so the early followers of Jesus, who were all Jewish, believed this as well. Those baptized into the original Jesus community were all Jews. However, something strange and unexpected happened. The book of Acts tells about Gentiles who heard the preaching of the Jewish apostles and who then manifested signs that the Holy Spirit had come upon them. The Gentiles who experienced the Holy Spirit requested baptism into the Jesus community. In one notable episode, the Apostle Philip meets a eunuch from Ethiopia and tells him about Jesus. The eunuch asks what prevents him from being baptized into the Jesus community (Acts 8:36). Philip could have replied, "Well, a lot! You are a Gentile and you are castrated so biblical law doubly excludes you." However, Philip was listening to the Holy Spirit, who was busy directing the Jesus community to take a radically different path.

In a vision, God told Peter to eat foods that the Bible instructed Jews not to eat. This would have produced a visceral reaction in Peter. It would be like leaving milk too long in the fridge and deciding to smell it to see if it is okay. You take a take a good sniff and your olfactory senses activate the disgust mechanism. You cannot help but jerk the jug away from you. The Old Testament declared lobsters and pigs unacceptable so obviously God did not accept the people who eat such foods. However, God told Peter not to think of Gentiles as "unclean" (ritually impure). Peter listened to God and baptized them. Then all hell broke loose in the fledgling church. Other Christians were outraged and used the Bible to point out to Peter that his innovative practice was against the clear teaching of the Bible. Those people do not belong in the Jewish church. If they want to use our water fountain, then they need to adopt the Jewish religion first. God has laid out the rules for who is in and out and if they want to be included then they have to follow the rules like everyone else. God does not allow exceptions. To gain admission to God's household they must live as we do. God will not accept them into the church unless (1) the males undergo circumcision, (2) people eat only the permitted foods, and (3) everyone keeps the Sabbath precisely the way we do it. One cannot be a citizen of God's country without these. After all, God ordained them. This is the social order God established. It is the way we have practiced our religion for hundreds of years. Who are you to change what God commanded?

In the year 50 CE Jewish followers of Jesus held a meeting in Jerusalem to discuss the matter. Acts 15 describes this meeting of as one of "great dissension." This was a heated debate about the widely accepted social order and traditional religion. The innovators, Peter and Paul, were going against what traditionalists took to be clear biblical teaching and hundreds of years of Jewish practice. They were attempting to change the social order in a way that seemed *obviously* wrong to many Christians. Churches throughout the Roman Empire hotly debated this topic. It threatened to split the tiny Christian community. Christians today seldom grasp the gravity of this dispute in the early church.

To defend his radical innovations Paul cherry picks texts from the Old Testament that speak favorably about Gentiles and he sets aside biblical teaching about Gentile exclusion. He is convinced that God is moving in a particular direction and claims that the love of God displayed in the life, death, and resurrection of Jesus means that the moral order governing how Jews and Gentiles related and who was, and was not, accepted by God needed revision. Tension arose because these are the very things that give life stability. Paul jettisons a number of highly important symbolic components of the early Christian social order. He says that Gentiles do not have to keep the Sabbath (one of the Ten Commandments), males do not have to be circumcised (a requirement to share in the Passover meal, according to Exodus 12:48), and they do not have to practice the dietary laws commanded by God in the Bible. Christians today take these changes for granted and have a difficult time understanding what the big deal was.

However, it was an earth-shaking matter at the time, because Peter and Paul were setting aside biblical commands as well as key practices that governed how Jews and Gentiles related in everyday life and worship. They wanted to make momentous changes that many argued would tear apart the social fabric and destroy the proper worship of God. Serious stuff indeed.

A great deal was on the line at that meeting in Jerusalem in the year 50. A common interpretation of the Bible and the taken-for-granted social order of the way Jews were accustomed to dealing with Gentiles were on the side of those who wanted to keep the traditional ways in place. Once you catch the magnitude of the situation, then it is stunning that the people at the meeting decided to make sweeping changes to traditional doctrines and practice. They announced that Gentiles did not have to become Jewish before they could join the Jesus community. Gentiles could live in the way of Jesus without having to keep the covenant regulations in the Old Testament. Paul says that Christ abolished the law because it separated humanity into Jews and Gentiles (Eph 2:15). There is only "one new humanity" now, he says. This is revolutionary because it abolishes the Authoritative boundary markers used to identify who is acceptable to God. It is worth noting that some Jewish Christians did not accept these changes. They preferred their traditional interpretation of Scripture. Yet, it is astonishing that most Jewish Christians embraced these radical changes to their religion. After all, they grew up believing the traditional view. This decision set aside some biblical teaching on the topic while highlighting other biblical teaching. The choice they made fundamentally changed the moral order of society. It is one of the most significant events in the history of any religion and it is, perhaps, the key reason for the amazing growth of Christianity over the next several centuries.[7]

TWO STRATEGIES TO REVISE OR SET ASIDE BIBLICAL TEACHING ON A TOPIC

Christians throughout history have followed the lead of biblical writers in revising and setting aside biblical teachings they find problematic. They have developed two main ways to accomplish this, using either criteria internal to the Bible or criteria external to the Bible.

7. See Stark, *Triumph*, 71–86, 413.

Inner Biblical Criteria

The first approach is to use some biblical teaching as the lenses through which to read other biblical texts. The community of faith identifies key texts that they use to guide their interpretation of other texts they find problematic. This is what Paul and Peter did to argue for Gentile inclusion into the Jesus community. Proponents of this method sometimes speak of "master" texts in the Bible that guide our way through the path of other Scriptures. Examples of guiding texts are Jesus' two greatest commandments: love God and love your neighbor and Paul's assertion that Christian communities override societal distinctions between Jew and Gentile, slave and freeperson, male and female (Gal 3:28). Christians have used these texts to justify setting aside other biblical texts that fall short of these ideals.

Sometimes disputes arise about which texts should guide our reading of other texts. For example, take the debate about whether or not God has changing emotions and whether God can change the divine mind. Some Christians point out the many dozens of biblical texts in which God, for instance, is said to grieve, have joy, and change God's mind. The other side appeals to biblical texts they claim are the "clear" teaching of Scripture such as Numbers 23:19 (God is not a human that God should change the divine mind). From such texts, they conclude that God has no changing mental or emotional states. This is not the place to settle these disputes. Rather, I simply note that Christians have always had disagreements about what to do with specific biblical texts and have regularly used some Scriptures to guide the interpretation of other texts. There are three variations of this approach.

The Criterion of Love

Augustine, an influential fourth-century pastor and thinker, used Jesus' teaching on love as the central guiding principle for reading Scripture. He says that when we come across morally objectionable statements in Scripture we should ask whether they promote love of God and neighbor. God seeks to inculcate love in people so anything in the Bible that goes against love can be set aside. The Old Testament defines adultery as a married woman having sex with a man who is not her husband. It was not considered adultery if husbands had sex with unmarried women. However, Augustine preached against this, saying it was a double standard and not a loving way to live. Augustine also said that when the Bible portrays God acting in unloving ways then we have the right to say God did not actually do what the biblical writers said God did. Other Christians use a similar approach when they say that Jesus is the clearest and best example of what God is like. Jesus is the lens through which one reads the Bible and if depictions of God commanding genocide or irrational violence in the Bible are incompatible with the character of Jesus, then we can be confident that God is not like this.[8] If the Old Testament teaches something that runs counter to Jesus, then Jesus wins—every time. This is so because Jesus is the very word of God (John 1:1) and the exact representation of what God is like (Heb 1:3).

We should note that Jesus himself was quite selective about which Scriptures to use. He ignores the texts about condemning people and stoning them for various infractions. For example, some people brought to Jesus a woman accused of adultery. The religious authorities said that the word of God demanded she be stoned to death but Jesus, the Word of God, rejected their Authoritative use of the Bible and showed grace to the woman. Jesus ignores all the exclusionary texts of Leviticus. He picks and chooses only the instruction to "love your neighbor as yourself" (Lev 19:18). When he announces his mission in Luke 4, he quotes Isaiah 61 about good news for the poor and release to the captives. However, he then stops mid-sentence and deliberately refuses to quote the rest of the sentence about divine vengeance. Jesus did this because it did not fit with his view of God as "Abba" who loves us. The Authoritatives accused Jesus of abolishing the law—it is all or nothing! However, Jesus shows how to use nurturing love to navigate Scripture responsibly.

Before Jesus and After Jesus

A widely used principle is to distinguish between what God expected *before* Jesus and what God desires *after* Jesus. Now that Jesus has come, all sorts of biblical laws are set aside. For instance, the followers of Jesus need not make grain or animal sacrifices in the Temple. Some Christians in the third century said that the biblical injunction against husbands having sex with their menstruating wives (Lev 15:19–24) was no longer in force after Jesus.

Early Christians strongly disagreed with each other about whether it was okay to paint pictures of Jesus. Some said only symbols such as fish, peacock, or anchor could be used, not any human form. After all, the Ten

8. See, for example, Boyd, *Cross Vision.*

Commandments prohibit images of God and Jesus is God. But other Christians painted images of Jesus as the good shepherd and events such as the raising of Lazarus. Painting images of the human Jesus became the norm. However, new disagreements arose over exactly how Jesus should look. Should he be a teenager or adult? Should he have a beard or not? What hair length and cut? Should he wear Palestinian or Roman clothing? Christians in different parts of world portrayed Jesus in many different ways. In the eighth century, things boiled over when a debate arose over the practice of bowing and praying in front of icons (paintings and statues of Jesus and saints). Many Christians were appalled at these practices because the Ten Commandments clearly says you shall have no idols (Exodus 20:4). Some Christians called the icons idols, so they went into churches with hammers and smashed the icons to pieces (which is how we got the word *iconoclast*). A major church council debated the matter in the year 787 and it decided that the Old Testament prohibition of icons was no longer binding now that God had come in the physical form of Jesus.

Follow the Trajectory

This variation admits that there are teachings that are less than ideal in the Bible but one finds in the Bible itself change and development on such topics. Some refer to this as "progressive revelation." The claim is that biblical texts about slavery, genocide, racism, and sexism become less and less acceptable over time. For instance, take the treatment of women in the Bible. Proponents of this strategy claim that one finds in the Bible an increasingly more humane attitude towards women. When we follow this trajectory, we can arrive at a position of full equality between females and males. Some abolitionists used this method to argue that the Bible moves from giving some protections to slaves to treating them as equals in Christ. They said that the goal of this trajectory was the end of slavery.

External Criteria

The second strategy for adapting or abandoning biblical teaching uses beliefs and values from one's era or culture to guide our reading of particular biblical texts. Once again, there are three variations of this approach.

If It Was Cultural, Then It Was Temporary

A popular interpretive maneuver is to classify as "cultural" any command that a Christian community considers irrelevant or objectionable. For instance, 1 Timothy 2:9 instructs Christian women not to wear braided hair, gold, pearls, or expensive clothes to worship. In America, women regularly wear these in church and feel no shame in doing so. This explicit teaching is set aside by saying it was relevant to that cultural context and is not applicable to ours. Another example of this is that for more than two thousand years Jews and Christians believed that part of what it meant to "honor your mother and father" (one of the Ten Commandments) was to marry the person they arranged for you. American Christians definitely do not believe that honoring your parents entails arranged marriages. Another example is the prohibition of tattoos (Lev 19:28). Though some Christians today practice this commandment, other Christians openly display tattoos despite the clear biblical prohibition. By classifying Old Testament moral teachings as "cultural" some Christians claim that prohibitions against tattoos, braided hair, and expensive clothing were okay for biblical times but we do not have to follow them today.

The Text Was Misinterpreted

This move acknowledges that Christians traditionally interpreted a biblical text in a particular way. However, we now realize that what they thought the Bible clearly taught is incorrect. For instance, Joshua 10:13 says that the sun stood still, which Christians for thousands of years took to mean that (a) the sun revolves around the earth and (b) the earth does not move. Martin Luther used this text to argue that Copernicus and Galileo were wrong. God knows the truth about nature and since the Bible is from God, the truth must be that the sun revolves around the earth. However, other Christians argued that past Christians had misunderstood this passage. John Calvin, for instance, held that though the Bible is from God, it is wrong to interpret such texts to be about science because biblical writers used ordinary human ideas such as the sun "sets." The motivation for revising the age-old interpretation of the text was, in fact, that these Christians were convinced that modern astronomy was correct so they read their Bibles in light of modern science.

Christians as far back as the thirteenth century said that the earth moves. They said that the biblical language about the sun moving and the earth not moving used a human perspective. Biblical writers believed that the sky was solid and did not know that stars were suns. Their cosmology was not what we believe today and God did not tell them otherwise.[9] Calvin used the idea of divine accommodation to say that God allowed biblical writers to use the views of nature accepted in their day.[10] Calvin said the Bible should not be used to determine what science can say. Instead, let the scientists figure out how nature works.

Some Biblical Writers Expressed Sentiments We No Longer Consider Moral

Sometimes, particular teachings of the Bible conflict with a moral standard of a society. For instance, Authoritative parents think that corporal punishment of children is important to make them morally strong. They usually defend this by appealing to the biblical commands regarding physical punishment of children. James Dobson (Focus on the Family) and other evangelicals claim that they practice what the Bible teaches on punishing children. However, they do not. The Bible says to beat children with a rod, strike children of any age, hit them up to forty times, leave welts on the back of the children, and punish in anger.[11] In our society these biblical practices are unacceptable and even illegal, so it not surprising that even those who claim to strictly follow biblical teaching on this matter do not actually do so.

The debate among Christians over the morality of slavery helpfully shows how both criteria internal to the Bible and criteria external from the Bible are used to revise or set aside biblical teaching on slavery. Slavery was one of the most contested moral issues in Christianity for centuries. One reason for this is that there is no Bible verse that clearly rejects slavery. Though the Bible does place some restrictions on how slaves are treated, it does not repudiate slavery. Paul orders slaves to obey their masters in everything (Col 3:22–25 and Eph 6:5–8) and Peter says slaves should obey even masters who treat them badly (2 Peter 2:18). In the United States, some Bible-believing Christians published biblical defenses of slavery.

9. See Walton, *Lost World.*

10. See McGrath, *Reformation*, 274–76.

11. See Webb, "A Redemptive," 232–34.

Other Bible-believing Christians argued for abolition. Aboliltionists were at a disadvantage since they could not provide any clear biblical teaching rejecting slavery. They had to resort to using the kinds of interpretive strategies discussed here such as the criterion of love, the overarching thrust of the Bible towards liberty, and the notion of basic human rights.[12] They had to use nuanced reasoning and sophisticated arguments. The proslavery Christians simply had to quote the Bible! A literal reading of Scripture supported slavery. They could claim that anyone who opposed slavery was not a "Bible-believing" Christian. Prior to the civil war, a Baptist minister in Virginia cited Exodus 21:20–22 to support slavery.[13] Exodus says, "When a slave owner strikes a male or female slave with a rod and the slave dies immediately, the owner shall be punished. But if the slave survives a day or two, there is no punishment; for the slave is his property." The pastor said that the Bible is "the divine authority" given by God and it grants slave owners the right to own slaves and the right to beat slaves with a rod that results in the death of the slave. *God* is the authority who commanded these laws. In 1862, a Methodist minister said the Confederate "cause is the cause of God, the cause of Christ, of humanity. It is a conflict of truth with error—of Bible with Northern infidelity—of pure Christianity with Northern fanaticism."[14]

Christians today find it difficult to understand how these Baptist and Methodist preachers could be so wrong about "pure Christianity" and what the Bible teaches. They fail to see that the proslavery position could point to chapter and verse supporting slavery, while the abolitionists had to use the internal and external strategies mentioned above to argue against the biblical texts that sanctioned slavery. One side had straightforward texts while the other side had to use sophisticated reasoning. Both sides read their Bible but the proslavery folks had the simpler position. After the slavery issue, American Christians debated whether to accept divorced persons into the church and then whether to allow interracial marriages. In both cases, Authoritatives used biblical texts along with cultural traditions to support their position.

In recent decades, several denominations have split over the issue of same-gender relationships. The patterns of reasoning in this debate are the same ones used in the debates over slavery, divorce, and interracial

12. For the biblical texts used by each side, see Noll, *Civil War*.

13. See Langston, *Exodus*, 209.

14. Noll, *Civil War*, 39.

marriage. Authoritatives argue that the Bible clearly condemns same-gender sexual relations. Either you agree with the Bible or you place your own reasoning above God's word. Christians who argue for acceptance of same-gender relationships use some of the strategies just discussed. Some argue the biblical texts have been misinterpreted because they do not deal with what we today call same-gender relationships. Instead, some biblical texts are about abusive power over others (such as male and female rape) while others address practices done in the worship of idols.[15] Others argue that just as some biblical teaching was used to set aside the biblical affirmation of slavery, so we should do the same for this issue. Using the biblical criterion of love, they argue we should now affirm same-gender relationships. In short, the same strategies used by abolitionists are available in this contentious debate. The key point here is that Nurturants are open to using these strategies on a range of topics but Authoritatives typically reject the use of such strategies on high profile issues such as slavery, divorce, and same-gender relationships. Yet, eventually Authoritatives did make use of these strategies for dealing with slavery and divorce and they quietly use these strategies on many other biblical texts they find problematic.

These are but a few of the many historical examples of Christians, from the time of Jesus, debating which biblical teachings to receive, which to revise, and which to reject. Throughout history, Christians have used these six strategies to adapt or abandon biblical teachings they found unacceptable. Authoritative believers like to proclaim that the authority of the Bible is an all-or-nothing affair. They talk a mean game but they do not actually practice what they preach. They never admit that they use these methods to set aside biblical teaching, but they do in fact. Augustine and most Christians in history have followed God's leading even while repudiating the all-or-nothing approach. They have developed judicious ways to sort through biblical teachings. They have acted responsibly when picking and choosing which biblical teachings to follow. The debates were not about whether it was legitimate to amend or set aside some biblical instructions. No, the debates were over which teachings to receive, which to revise, and which to reject. Christian communities have repeatedly asked, "What would Jesus do?" in order to decide which texts to adopt, which to adapt, and which to abort. They looked to the center of the faith to figure out what it means to practice love regarding contentious issues such as slavery. Churches would be better off if they just fessed up and admitted that such debates are an

15. See Gushee, *Changing*, and Gnuse, "Seven Gay Texts."

inherent part of the Christian life. Being up-front about this matter would help Christians make sense of the variation we observe among Christian communities. Of course, disagreements arise about whether a biblical teaching is loving or just. It is normal for Christian communities to have contentious debates, which may take decades to resolve—particularly those that involve changes to long-standing cultural traditions.

CONCLUSION

As we seek to live out the Christian faith in new settings, we need to use the resources available to us. Three key resources are the Bible, church traditions (plural), and contemporary learning. The Bible does many things but most importantly, it furnishes a guide to the center of Christianity—Jesus. Second, we also pay attention to the agreements and disagreements in Christian history. Traditions help us see how previous Christians interpreted and applied biblical teachings and how they integrated this with the best learning of their day. Third, Christians have always made use of what they took to be true and ethical derived from the best knowledge available at the time. Christian have always had conflicts over what to do when a biblical teaching is in tension with what contemporary Christians consider correct. When this happens we need to dialogue. We respect the Bible as a means of grace that nurtures Christian communities on the path of love. At the same time, we also take seriously the idea that biblical texts are inescapably enmeshed in human cultures that took particular cultural values and practices, such as slavery, for granted. It is a conversation between Christian communities and the Bible. Christian communities rightly regard the Bible as a sacred text that shapes their identity. Yet, they also see that some biblical teachings are out of line with the best reasoning we have available on a topic. Therefore, we need to acknowledge that it is a two-way street and engage in honest dialogue about our differences.

We need to follow the lead of folks such as Paul and Peter, who reflected on what the gospel of Jesus meant for their day and age. We should imitate their practice of using Jesus as the focal point to think about how to follow God in our day and age rather than simply mimic their precise words. They brought about a religious and social revolution regarding how Gentiles were treated. After centuries of debate, Christians renounced slavery. Both of these involved setting aside particular biblical teaching, highlighting other biblical teachings, and transforming important parts of the social order of the day. These changes were difficult but they did not abandon biblical authority or destroy the society, as some claimed would happen. Recognizing the need to responsibly question long-standing practices and sometimes revise the social order comes more naturally to Nurturant Christians.

7

STYLES OF RELATING

Some years ago, I taught an adult Sunday school class on various theological topics. My style of teaching was the same I used in my college classroom—a range of Christian views on a topic were presented along with the biblical texts and theological reasons used to support each position. Then, questions about each view followed. I did not tell the class which positions I favored and went out of my way to explain and defend views with which I personally disagreed. I tried to present them as a proponent of that position would. People loved the format and attendance grew from ten to around forty, so we had to move the class into a larger room. That is when the pastor took note and asked to meet with me. He had serious concerns about the class and decided that I should no longer teach the class. His main objection was that I was not teaching the single correct view on each theological topic. He worried that people would flounder in their faith instead of being firmly rooted in the one true position. What was the one correct position on each topic? The views he held, of course.

A few years later, I was teaching a course on world religions at an evangelical college. A student in the class went to the dean to complain, "Dr. Sanders is teaching Hinduism so well that I'm worried some students may convert." When the dean defended my pedagogy the student said that the purpose of the course should not be to help students understand each religion. The point is not to see things from another perspective. Rather, the only reason to study other religions was to learn why they are wrong. The student left the dean's office dismayed that he would not correct this horrible approach to education.

These two stories capture some of the differences in the "cognitive style" of the Nurturant and Authoritative approaches. Cognitive style involves topics such as whether we value perspective-taking, can tolerate some other views, and whether we hold our convictions with humility or dogmatism.

NURTURING COGNITIVE STYLE

A Nurturing way of life believes it is virtuous to foster dialogue, perspective-taking, empathy for others, humility, and tolerance. The ability to correctly understand a position different from one's own and make sense of the reasons why someone would hold that position is what I have sought to model to my students for decades. After one course, a student thanked me saying that he now understood the Calvinism he learned in his church much better than before. Despite the fact that I personally strongly disagree with this theological view, I was glad the student found my presentations of the position clear and accurate.

Social scientists observe that those with a Nurturing orientation think of life as complex and so are more comfortable with shades of gray and nuanced statements. Though some things may be black and white, many aspects of life are not easily decided. In addition, they want to be fair so they desire balanced and accurate information on topics. They value learning about other cultures and peoples in order to enlarge their understanding of the world. Children are encouraged to question things in appropriate ways and parents want them to learn to think for themselves instead of merely mimicking what others have said. The journalist Fareed Zakaria is an immigrant who treasures the American educational system over that of his native India. He says that American universities excel at producing the vast majority of the creative scientists, entrepreneurs, innovators, and business leaders because they value an education that requires students to think outside the box.[1] Universities in China and India focus on rote memorization and following the rules while American schools teach independent thinking and following ideas with merit even if this sometimes means challenging what authorities have said. The "liberal" in a liberal arts education means to liberate students from a regimented and narrow approach to one that engages diverse approaches and perspectives including mathematics,

1. Zakaria, *In Defense.*

history, religion, and science in order to be well informed, think for one's self, and live a meaningful life.

There is an old adage: "To understand someone, you need to walk a mile in their shoes." To do this requires empathy and perspective-taking. The Christian doctrine of the incarnation shows that God fully engages in perspective-taking by walking in our shoes. God learned what it was like to be in our place. Philosophers speak of God's "great-making" properties but they seldom include empathy and perspective-taking in the list. However, God is love and part of what it means to treat others as we want to be treated is to try to understand things from their perspective. Research shows a number of benefits for those with strong skills in perspective-taking.[2] People are more trusting and cooperative, use fewer stereotypes to understand others, and identify discrimination when it occurs. When others perceive you as trying to understand them, they are more likely to trust and help you. Unfortunately, research also shows that people in leadership positions are less likely to practice "walking in another's shoes." Leaders with Nurturing values are more likely to be aware of this tendency and so take steps to ensure that people in their businesses, congressional districts, and churches have a voice. Empathy and perspective-taking help us listen to the concerns of others in church and society.

AUTHORITATIVE COGNITIVE STYLE

Those with Authoritative values tend to prefer black and white thinking without need of qualifications.[3] They have a high need for cognitive closure—for certainty that they are correct.[4] There is a clear right and wrong way to do things. There are definitive boundaries demarcating whatever is right. Truth is absolute and independent of historical periods and cultures. This leads to inflexible thinking. Authoritatives tend to hold their worldview as an unalterable truth and are significantly more prone to confirmation bias and rejecting empirical truth.[5] They exhibit an unwillingness

2. For a summary of the research, see Zorwick, "Using Debate."

3. An excellent study on the Authoritative style is Hetherington and Weiler, *Authoritarianism.*

4. In evangelicalism, this is one of the motivations for the doctrine of inerrancy—there are no errors in the Bible. Inerrantists posit an absolutely certain strong foundation from which to build what they consider failsafe theologies.

5. See Hetherington and Weiler, *Prius,* 141–42 and the Baylor Religion Survey,

to examine information that might challenge their views. When someone does challenge their views, Authoritatives have a tendency to become more interested in finding one-sided information that reinforces what they already believe rather than locating balanced information. Authoritative theologians trust only other Authoritative scholars so they tend to be insular in what they read. For instance, when I taught at evangelical colleges I was sharply criticized for citing non-evangelical scholars in my work even though these people were rock stars in the field. The only reason to learn the views outside your tribe is to show why they are wrong.

In addition, Authoritatives prefer a uniform and unchanging social order. The boundaries of a good society are clearly marked so everyone knows what is acceptable and gate keeping is an important activity to preserve social stability. Authoritatives are intolerant of those perceived as violating time-honored norms. Conformity to traditional ideas is valued. Children should learn the correct ideas and not be exposed to other forms of thinking except to show why those ideas are wrong. People must not question the correct views. Fear motivates the need for certainty. Changing one's mind on any traditional teaching is dangerous. If one questions entrenched beliefs, then one's entire worldview may crumble. Correct thinking means to align one's own ideas and values with conventional ideals. In addition, they tend to be more parochial, focused on their in-group and less interested in other cultures. Finally, they are more at ease with a single "strong" autocratic leader who takes control and tells others what they should do. There is less of a concern to uphold democratic values in organizational life. Making sure that everyone has a voice is not a high priority.

COMPARISONS

In terms of religion, both types imitate who they understand God to be (see chapter 4). They treat others the way they believe God treats them. The Nurturant God graciously listens to others, uses flexible strategies, and sometimes changes the divine mind. The Authoritative God does not listen to others or modify the divine plan. The Nurturing way encourages a "pilgrim" theology while the Authoritative orientation leads to a "fortress" theology. A pilgrim on a quest has a destination but anticipates making adjustments along the way. Pilgrims expect their religious experience to grow and change. We have some general directions about our destination

---

"American Values."

but no detailed map with step-by-step directions. Though many saints have tread the path before us and we can learn from their testimonies, we still need to be resourceful and develop problem-solving skills. Improvisation is required along the journey. That is why we need wisdom and not just knowledge of facts. Pilgrim theology is aware that our knowledge is always partial so pilgrims expect questions to arise. Pilgrim or quest religion involves curiosity and an openness to new ideas. It does not mean one accepts every new idea; just that one is not close-minded.

One psychological study investigated people's attachment to God and their preference for a quest or fortress religion.[6] It asked people how often they worry whether or not God is pleased with them and whether they fear God does not accept them when they do wrong. Those with a secure attachment to God affirmed traditional Christian beliefs but were willing to explore theological ideas and had greater tolerance for Christians who held different views. They also had greater peace and less anxiety in their spiritual lives. Those who believe in the Authoritative God exhibited a conditional attachment to God and were fearful of displeasing God if they inquired into different theological ideas. They were also less tolerant of Christians who held different theological views.

Political scientists distinguish between "bonding" and "bridging" social relationships.[7] Bonding occurs when you associate with your in-group—those who look and think like you do. It provides a sense of place where you feel you belong. Bridging happens when you interact with those who are different ethnically, religiously, or politically. Those who spend time only with members of their tribe exhibit distrust towards outsiders. Getting to know someone outside your group builds understanding and trust even though you do not agree with them about everything. Bridging with people who are different religiously produces trust and concern for their well-being. Authoritatives prefer bonding to bridging while Nurturing people value both.

Those with an Authoritative orientation exhibit unwavering faith in their position and prefer not to reflect on different points of view. One study used a "defensive theology scale" to measure the degree to which Christians believed God furnished them with privileged information, has a special plan for their lives, that chance events do not happen, and the

6. Beck, "God."

7. See Putnam and Campbell, *American Grace*, 531–32 and 547–48.

like.[8] It turns out that those with an Authoritative understanding of God were more defensive about their theological positions and held greater in-group bias. They are strongly convinced their group has the correct views and see no need to question them or consider other views. In addition, they fear what God might do to them if they changed any of their positions. Nurturant Christians, on the other hand, feel secure in God and so are open to new understandings over time. They believe they hold the right views (who doesn't?) but are open to revising their positions in light of new information.

When someone expresses a different view, Authoritative believers are fond of asking; "But what if you are wrong?" The implication is that God does not take kindly to people holding incorrect views. Believing that God will send you to hell for considering different theological ideas naturally produces anxiety and fear of being wrong. Authoritatives see questions about traditional beliefs and practices as a threat. Of course, some Nurturants are dogmatic but this attitude runs counter to the core values of the Nurturing approach. The good news is that people can change. Take the case of a young woman raised in the Westboro Baptist Church, a tiny congregation that teaches, "It is simple: God loves us and hates you."[9] She gradually changed her views and left that group. It began, she says, when someone showed accepting love to her online. She expected hatred from outsiders but when someone responded to her messages of hate with empathy, she began to change. In order for changes like this to occur, we need to help Authoritatives build bridges so that they begin to see the perspective of others. Some churches, community organizers, and media outlets bring different people together so that genuine conversations can begin.[10] It takes time and help from others to bring about a transformation from the Authoritative to the Nurturing way of life, but it happens.

The Apostle Paul said that Christians "know in part" and "see dimly" (1 Cor 13:9–12). Proponents of the Nurturant God are aware that there is always more to know and that our languages and cultures shape our views.[11] Nurturants hold their convictions as true, yet they hold their views with a degree of humility. Even our cherished understandings of what is

---

8. Beck, "Defensive." See also Sandage et al., "Calvinism."

9. Froese and Bader, *America's Four Gods*, 79.

10. See Hetherington and Weiler, *Prius*, 84–86. For some success stories of bridging, see Sample, *Working Class*.

11. For numerous examples of these ideas, see Sanders, *Theology*.

true and moral may need revision as new light shines on a topic. Believers in the Authoritative God, however, are the most absolutist and dogmatic.[12] Authoritative Christians often claim that there are only two options: absolute certainty or complete relativism. Either we have the clear-cut truth and we can prove it, or it is "anything goes." As a result, they live in fear of being wrong and tend to be close-minded to information that may challenge their convictions. The truth of the matter is that certainty and total relativism are not the only two options. We can affirm the limitations of human knowing and still take stands on issues. We make a case for our views with the best information we have available and seek to persuade others. We do this knowing that we may need to revise and change some of our thinking in the future. We can hold convictions about what God wants us to do while also being aware that we only have a partial understanding. Even our grasp of divine revelation is limited, which is one reason we need others to help us see things we have missed. This is not relativism but humility.

In a previous chapter, I mentioned the pastor who asked me, "Why did you place a question mark where God put a period?" Authoritatives tend to allow no room between what they believe on a particular teaching and what God thinks. That means that when you question their view, you are questioning God. I cannot tell you how many times people have accused me of questioning God when what I was doing was questioning the theology of a particular group. However, since they equate their doctrines with God's beliefs, Authoritatives are not open to a conversation. Many years ago, I taught at a college where a cabal of trustees plotted to get me dismissed. The president of the college wanted me to address the board, but this group forbade it. According to their Authoritative values, it was not important to listen to what I had to say. What was important was to enforce what this group of trustees believed to be theologically correct. The president arranged for me to meet with some trustees and clergy but I soon discovered that they were not interested in dialogue. My attempts to help them understand my views fell on deaf ears. They simply wanted me gone and made several power plays to intimidate the president.

KUDZU RELIGION

When driving around the southern United States you notice a tremendous diversity of trees and plants, but then you come to places where everything

12. Froese and Bader, *America's Four Gods*, 67, 149, 153.

is uniform and monochrome. Kudzu is a vine that chokes out all biodiversity and kills off everything else until it is the only plant left. It covers trees and fields until all other life dies. Kudzu religion does the same. It chokes out all diversity of Christian belief and practice. Everyone has to think the same way and conform to the beliefs and behaviors handed down from the top. Kudzu religion is committed to the purity of the church so that everyone is alike. It becomes a monopoly religion.

In the early centuries of Christianity there were general agreements about the importance of baptism and the Lord's Supper, yet there was a great deal of diversity about what they meant and exactly how to perform the rituals. At least from the time of the emperor Constantine, many have enforced kudzu religion requiring strict conformity in doctrine and practice. During the Protestant Reformation state churches developed. If one lived in Scandinavia, then one had to practice Lutheranism. If you lived in France, then you had to be Roman Catholic. Christians persecuted and killed one another for belonging to the wrong tribe. The Anabaptists (rebaptizers) believed in the separation of church and state and that Christians are supposed to love even those outside their tribe. Small wonder that all the other Christians hated them. Some Anabaptists were "re-baptized" by wrapping them in chains and drowning them in rivers to purify the church of these blasphemous ideas. In nineteenth-century America, many Protestants uttered harsh rhetoric against Catholics and claimed that American society would vanish unless Catholicism was expunged from our great nation. In Philadelphia Protestants killed priests and nuns because they wanted to use a different translation of the Bible in public schools. Eventually, religious liberty won out over the attempts to make America a mono-religious nation.

Rodney Stark notes that though monopoly churches have often existed they cannot sustain themselves because no single church can adequately meet the interests of all people.[13] The monopolies stay in power only by repressing and punishing those who develop alternative beliefs or practices. Diversity is a threat so monopolies work hard to exterminate variation. One doctrine, one practice, one interpretation. So kudzu Christians burned other Christians alive or cut out their tongues so they could not talk about divergent ideas or practices. The same attitudes are alive today. One author wrote that he prayed God would kill me for espousing such an obviously wrong view of God. A group of pastors and trustees used all sorts of

13. Stark, *Triumph*, 309.

nefarious means to have me fired from my college. In the meetings with them, I had the eerie feeling that if they could cut out my tongue or burn me at the stake they would. It is sad that I was grateful for a secular government that allows kudzu Christians to fire others but prevents them from putting others to the fire.

Authoritative believers are predisposed towards kudzu religion. The concerns for purity and conformity coupled with the fear of divine punishment for being wrong incline them to enforce a monopolistic church that eliminates all diversity. Nurturant believers, on the other hand, favor a constrained pluralism in which a number of views and practices are accepted. They tolerate a range of positions even while they affirm specific views. Because we live in specific communities, we will favor particular forms of worship and piety. Nurturant Christians will take stands on what they believe is the best view or practice yet, they will not seek to impose kudzu religion.

The different cognitive styles of Nurturants and Authoritatives sheds light on many of the "culture wars" in American history.[14] During periods of change, such as when Catholics wanted a voice in society or when Victorian homogeneity was losing its grip, those with Authoritative values become fearful of what would happen when people stop practicing a traditional social convention. Authoritatives protest the loss of their right to decide who is a true American and which cultural practices are enforced. In an attempt to restore their control, they blame others, such as Catholics and Asians, for what they call a "decline" in America. They say such folks are not genuine Americans and so do not belong here. It is like the food laws of the Old Testament—it is about purity. Only fish with fins and scales are fish. Lobsters are not true fish and so you are not to eat them. In the same way, Catholics are not genuine Christians and gays are not true humans. God has determined what is pure and such groups are impure. They are unacceptable to God. Authoritatives have used all sorts of horrible rhetoric to promote the fear of the destruction of their version of the American way of life. For example, they accused Thomas Jefferson of being a secret Muslim who would destroy America if he became president. Does that ring a bell? It is what many Authoritatives said about Barak Obama. The Authoritative political playbook repeats the same accusations with new names. Decades ago, states passed anti-Catholic measures to preserve a Protestant America. In addition, states enacted laws prohibiting teaching foreign languages in

14. The following comments are indebted to the insightful book by Prothero, *Why*.

public schools to protect traditional American values. This is a fear-based religion. In contrast, Nurturants spoke of hope for a better America in which liberty would flourish. They promoted democracy to ensure that all groups had a voice in the public square. Today, the issues have changed but the Authoritatives continue to use the same tactics of fear and demonizing those who threaten kudzu society.

In religion, Authoritatives draw sharp boundary lines, claim to be the only genuine Christians, and drop tons of rhetorical bombs on anyone who questions them. Nurturing Christians do not fear variation so they are more likely to value and learn from different perspectives. Today, it is difficult to imagine Christians killing one another over which Bible translation to read in public schools. But we did. Kudzu religion opposes religious liberty.

EVANGELICALS

In America, there are both Nurturant and Authoritative evangelicals. For the past few decades, Authoritative evangelicals have received most of the media attention and they have influenced many from traditionally Nurturing denominations to adopt their Authoritative cognitive style along with some of their doctrines. White evangelicals score significantly higher on the Authoritative scale compared to Catholics, other Protestants, or Jews.[15] They eschew the notion that Christians should always be reforming their beliefs and practices because they already have the correct views.[16] Their own beliefs and practices are sacrosanct, which is why they commit the "sin of certainty."[17]

Evangelical publishers have produced a large number of "multi-views" books. Such books present three to five different positions Christians hold on topics such as baptism or the atonement. A proponent of each view writes a chapter explaining and giving reasons for the view. At the end of each chapter, the other authors state their agreements and disagreements. I have contributed to two such books and in each, two of the Authoritative contributors refused to follow the accepted format. They simply assume their view is the "clear" teaching of the Bible and the only real position held by Christians historically. In at least one case, the publisher pleaded with that author to explain and defend his position but he refused, saying

15. Hetherington and Weiler, *Authoritarianism*, 59–60.

16. On this and the following points, see Olson, *Reformed*.

17. Enns, *Sin of Certainty*.

if he followed the format it would make his position on the topic simply one of several. The very existence of dozens of multi-views books ought to show evangelicals that responsible Christians have held a range of views on many topics.

The Nurturant approach is more comfortable with a "constrained pluralism" of views. This is the idea that though one is convinced that a particular position on a topic is the best one to hold, one is aware that other faithful Christians disagree on the matter. It is not "anything goes" or "you have your opinion and I have mine." Rather, it is the acknowledgment that genuine Christians hold a range of views (a limited diversity) on a topic and that proponents of each view have reasons for their position that not all Christians find persuasive. Authoritative evangelicals fiercely proclaim that position X is the correct position on a given topic. The multi-views books show that evangelicals have not been able to agree on what the single correct position is. They reveal that evangelicals actually hold what I call a "constrained pluralism" on most topics, including the ordination of women, the nature of God, and spirituality. Nurturants are comfortable with this situation but the Authoritatives tend to be upset that views other than the correct "one" are included in the books or are presented in classes as genuine options. That is why the pastor and the student mentioned at the beginning of the chapter objected to my teaching, which presented the variation of Christian views on each topic.

Authoritative evangelicals tend to believe that their own theological beliefs developed free from cultural influences. A favorite tactic is to accuse theologians who hold different beliefs of being contaminated by American values. Their own minds are pure and so are able to find the unvarnished truth—truth that is free from all historical or social context. They love to say that each of their theological positions is the "clear teaching" of the Bible. This means that the true position is obvious. Hence, if you disagree with their view, you are either corrupted by culture, willfully sinful, or just plain stupid. One would think that their own multi-views books would show them that the "clear" teaching is not as clear as they think.

Authoritative evangelicals are obsessed with identifying the theological boundary lines for who is in and who is out. They vigilantly patrol the borders to prevent ideas deemed undesirable from entering and are intolerant of those perceived as crossing the line. When evangelical pastor Rob Bell published his best-selling *Love Wins*, to suggest that God's love may not give up on wayward children after death, there were acrimonious denunciations. Authoritative evangelicals ripped it for challenging what they took to be a rejection of the obvious and clear teaching of the Bible about salvation. In response to publications defending the idea that God is open and responsive to what people do, Authoritative evangelicals published titles such as *The Battle for God* and *God Under Fire*. They love to use warfare language and they readily resort to harsh, angry denunciations. One theologian wrote that my notions of God would destroy the church. Fear of this perceived threat led one professor to get his students to give my book a low rating on Amazon in order to dissuade others from reading it.

Over the past twenty-five years, I have written on several theological topics. One thing that surprised me was when Authoritative evangelicals failed to state my views correctly or did not consider ways my positions could easily address their questions. These were smart people with doctoral degrees. I could accurately articulate their position and think about how they would likely respond to an objection. Why did they not do this with my work? I now know that perspective-taking is not a virtue regularly practiced by Authoritatives. Given their cognitive style, they presume their views are correct and tend to react to challenges with dismissal or misrepresentations.

CONCLUSION

The Nurturing and Authoritative ways of life have very different cognitive styles. Those with an Authoritative orientation value conformity and uniformity, clear boundaries, certitude in their convictions, and have a legacy of kudzu religion that chokes out all diversity in doctrine and practice. Nurturing Christians have a secure relationship with God. This enables them to live as pilgrims and deal with times of uncertainty. Questioning established views is appropriate. They value bridging relationship with outsiders. These traits enable them to trust others and preserve theological biodiversity. They practice perspective taking and empathy. They take stands on what they believe is correct but hold their convictions with humility. They allow for a constrained pluralism on many beliefs and practices. Once again, we see that Nurturing Christianity leads to superior forms of spirituality and better relationships.

8

IN HIS STEPS

"Wait. Wait. Before we talk any more I need to know if you have any moral standards." I was shocked and a bit annoyed by my friend's remark. We were having a conversation about issues in American society such as income inequality and what I was saying sounded to my friend like I had no morals whatsoever. Of course I have moral standards! How could this person so misunderstand what I was saying? Then I remembered that I was talking to someone with Authoritative values. For them, questioning their moral absolutes meant I must be a moral relativist—a permissive parent, without any standards. Proponents of the Authoritative view tend to judge any approach other than their own as having no standards whatsoever. The Nurturant approach does have moral standards but does not hold them in the same way as the Authoritative view does.

THE NURTURANT APPROACH TO MORALITY

Relationships are central to the Nurturing way of life and moral decisions occur in the context of relationships to God, family, and others. The primary goal is to maintain healthy relationships. Moral rules have a role in this but the rules exist for the sake of the relationships, the relationships do not exist for the sake of the rules. Jesus said that the Sabbath was made to help humans, humans were not created to obey the Sabbath (Mark 2:27). Moral rules function as guides for how to behave in typical situations. A maxim such as "do not lie" tells you what to do in most situations but life is sometimes more complex, so we need to develop skills to know what we should do in circumstances that are not prototypical.[1] When the Nazis ruled Germany, it was illegal to hide Jews and other "undesirables" who contaminated German ideals. Some people broke the law and sheltered them. When the Gestapo investigated, the people lied to the authorities. Dietrich Bonhoeffer was a German theologian executed by the Nazis. In his essay on telling the truth, he says that telling the truth is not about following a rule but, rather, acquiring the skill to apply what God wants to accomplish in this situation.

To acquire this skill, it is helpful to learn what exemplary people did in various situations. Stories allow our minds to run simulations about different settings and consider various scenarios about what to do. Exemplary people manifest virtues that we seek to inculcate in our lives. Yet we do not simply mimic their behavior. Rather, we have to improvise to apply the virtues in different situations. Moral reasoning involves much more than simply memorizing a set of rules for every situation. Wisdom is required to apply virtues and maxims so that we do what is best for that relationship. Micah 6:8 expresses some important aspects of a Nurturant moral vision: do justice, love kindness, and walk humbly with God.

There are moral maxims that most, if not all, human cultures have held throughout history. The Ten Commandments lists some of these: do not murder, do not steal, and do not give false testimony. Ancient Near Eastern legal codes had these same rules long before the Bible was written. These maxims are very general in nature and cover most of the situations in which we find ourselves. They are general guidelines for life but they may not apply to some situations. In addition, ancient culture shaped the moral instructions in the Bible. God worked with ancient Israelites whose culture assumed many particular values. One implication of this approach is that morals given to ancient Israel may not be directly applicable or even considered moral in other times and places. For instance, take the commandment that if a man rapes a woman who was not engaged to be married then he has to marry the woman and never divorce her (Deut 22:28–9). Even if this made sense in ancient Israel, Christians have decided it is not an acceptable moral practice any longer.

1. For a fuller account of this approach see Sanders, *Theology*, chapter 6.

THE AUTHORITATIVE APPROACH TO MORALITY

Moral reasoning is quite different according to the Authoritative approach. Here, there are clear guidelines that specify what is right and wrong. Maxims such as do not murder, do not lie, and do not steal articulate in plain terms how to behave in all situations. Children need to learn these clear and straightforward rules and obey them without exception. We do not need wisdom, just knowledge of the rules. The maxims are universals that define right and wrong for all times and cultures. What is truly moral never changes and does not vary from one culture to the next. They are moral absolutes that can never be broken. They apply in every situation regardless of the relationships involved. Augustine, for example, said that one should never lie under any circumstances. The maxims are God-given so they can never be changed in any way. One does not mess with God's orders. The Ten Commandments summarize a number of these moral absolutes and the Ten Commandments have symbolic importance for Authoritatives. Hence, they put plaques and monuments of the Ten Commandments in schools and on the grounds of state houses.

In addition, Authoritatives believe people are morally weak and need to develop moral strength to survive in a competitive and dangerous world. We must not coddle people if they are to grow. A student told me about a friend named Tom that he was helping. Tom's mother had suffered a brain aneurysm and in the following weeks Tom experienced an emotional decline. He was having a rough go in life. The spiritual mentor to my student advised him: "God gives us hard situations in life so that we grow. Tom is suffering because he is not strong enough. You should not help him because your assistance will rob Tom of the opportunity to grow." In other words, if you really want to help your friend, do not coddle him. He must overcome the problem on his own or suffer the consequences.

SOCIAL ORDER

The social order of society involves the customary ways people interact. It includes everything from offering a person visiting your home something to drink to whether or not we consider sexual harassment acceptable in the workplace. Martin Luther and other reformers introduced significant changes to worship in the sixteenth century. One such change was having the entire congregation sing in church rather than just the male choir.

This meant that in the streets one could now hear women's voices. Many traditionalists were outraged at this. The religious protesters made other changes as well. They got rid of paintings and statues of saints in churches. Clergy no longer performed "last rites" for the dead and ended the practice called "churching" for women after childbirth. Such practices had reassured Christians that God accepted them. Protestants made lots of changes to religious practices in a relatively short time span, which left many people longing for the good old days when people worshipped in traditional ways that bound society together. Many folks were pleased when Emperor Charles V had thousands of Protestants beheaded and burned women alive to restore God's moral order.

Sometimes people idealize a historical period and are not aware of the shortcomings of that era. As I write this passage, people are setting off fireworks for the Fourth of July holiday. Americans rightly celebrate Independence Day and its focus on liberty. Yet liberty originally was not applied to all people in America and our history is riddled with the struggle of specific groups to claim liberty for themselves. Leaders such as Abraham Lincoln and Martin Luther King Jr. extolled the virtues of the Declaration of Independence and the Constitution. Yet, they also realized that America had not yet arrived at her destination. In the Gettysburg Address Lincoln said the nation had "unfinished work" because the US Constitution legalized slavery. It is a good document but he thinks it needs to be improved. Lincoln appeals to a core value of America enshrined not in the Constitution but in the earlier Declaration of Independence: "that all men are created equal." He speaks of a nation "conceived in liberty" and claims that America has fallen short of this ideal due to the slavery of blacks. Hence, he calls for "a new birth of freedom," which involved changing the Constitution in order to be true to America's guiding values. Many Authoritatives were outraged. Some accused Lincoln of redefining America because it was obvious that the original intent of the Declaration did not include blacks.[2] I believe that Authoritatives today would continue to take exception to Lincoln's reasoning that blacks should be included in the Declaration's "all men are created equal" clause because 74 percent of them affirm an approach to interpretation that says what the author meant is the only legitimate meaning.[3]

In his "I Have a Dream" speech, King stood in front of the Lincoln memorial and, like Lincoln before him, spoke of unfinished work in America.

2. See Prothero, *American Bible*, 332–33.

3. Hetherington and Weiler, *Prius*, 34.

"When the architects of our republic wrote the magnificent words of the Constitution and the Declaration of Independence, they were signing a promissory note to which every American was to fall heir. This note was a promise that all men, yes, black men as well as white men, would be guaranteed the 'unalienable Rights' of 'Life, Liberty and the pursuit of Happiness.' It is obvious today that America has defaulted on this promissory note, insofar as her citizens of color are concerned. Instead of honoring this sacred obligation, America has given the Negro people a bad check, a check which has come back marked 'insufficient funds.'" King believed that the authors of America's founding documents should be interpreted as an encompassing vision of liberty and opportunity—the check was for everyone rather than only for white people.

In subsequent periods, there were other tumultuous issues which pitted the value of liberty against Authoritative sensibilities. One was the movement to allow women the right to vote. Many religious Authoritatives said that granting full rights of participation in government and society to women was a clear sign of moral decay—departing from God's ordained way of ordering society. Even as recent as 2016, about 50 percent of Authoritatives said that women should "return to their traditional roles."[4] In addition, white Authoritatives in American resisted fair housing laws, interracial marriage, and desegregated schools. In particular, the civil rights movement made a lot of folks uncomfortable that things were changing too fast. Many people thought the way things had been for hundreds of years was what God ordained so they opposed these changes. In 1963 seven prominent white Christian pastors and a rabbi published a letter in the *Birmingham News* criticizing the civil rights movement for demanding social changes for blacks too fast. They said people needed to observe "law and order" to prevent "hatred and violence."[5] They said that if blacks would simply wait for the courts to make changes instead of demonstrating in the streets, then everything would be fine. King responded with his famous "Letter From a Birmingham Jail." He writes: "We have waited for more than 340 years for our constitutional and God given rights" and says they are still waiting for public schools to obey the law and desegregate.[6] For Authoritatives, protesting showed disrespect to those in authority and challenged traditional social norms.

4. Hetherington and Weiler, *Prius*, 38.
5. Carpenter et al., "Call for Unity."
6. King, "Letter."

People with an Authoritative orientation often think that God ordained the moral and social practices that have been around a long time. For centuries, Christians thought that God selected particular males to rule the land. The "divine right of kings" meant that God, not the people, selected the rulers. When the Christian writer John Locke claimed that ordinary people had the right to rebel against kings and establish their own democratic governments, some said this was opposed to God's way of doing things.

Social scientists find that a key Authoritative value is the strong desire to preserve social norms and institutions that have become "traditional" in society. During the first 250 years of Christianity, there were sporadic persecutions of Christians by Roman leaders. They accused Christians of "hating humanity" and being atheists for not worshipping the gods. Repeating these charges from household to household helped make Christians a despised minority. After all, Christians did not attend the games like "genuine" Romans did and they denied that the Roman gods even existed. Sometimes the government passed laws requiring Christians to show proper loyalty to Rome by making a public offering to the emperor. Other laws prohibited Christians from holding public office and serving in the military. Because Christians contaminated Roman society, they suffered torture, disfigurement, confiscation of property, and sometimes death. Why did emperors such as Decius and Diocletian order the persecution of Christians? Romans felt their society had declined and the emperors wanted to restore the glory of Rome. Christians were the cause of the decline because they lacked true Roman values and did not affirm the narrative of what made Rome great. They blamed Christians for floods, epidemics, and invasions. This made sense because Roman religion was important to the foundation of the Roman Empire. The Roman gods gave their blessing to Rome but these deities were now punishing society because the Christians failed to worship the gods. Because of this, Christians were actually accused of being atheists! The well-being of society required a return to the "traditional" religion and rejection of Christianity in order to make Rome great again.

In the past two centuries, Christians divided over whether to make changes to the social order regarding slavery, civil rights, and women's rights. Those who embraced the Authoritative view tried to uphold the time-tested morality of slavery, segregation, and male rule. Religious Authoritatives, and evangelicals in particular, widely opposed the civil rights movement. On the other hand, people with Nurturing values believed society needed significant changes in order to be in harmony with God's values.

What are we to do when Christians disagree on matters that each side feels strongly about? Both sides believe the other affirms an immoral position, so it is not a matter of finding a middle ground. From the birth of the church, Christians have disagreed strongly about pivotal matters (see chapter 7). They have disagreed about whether or not Gentiles (non-Jews) could be members of the Jesus community without them first becoming Jewish. Christians were at odds for centuries over slavery. Today, we do not feel the tension our predecessors felt regarding Gentile inclusion or slavery. The "correct" position on these topics seems obvious to us now. But it was not obvious at the time. Granting Gentiles full inclusion in the Jesus community, granting blacks civil rights, and allowing women to vote were extremely contentious issues at the time. Today, it is hard to imagine that many Christians once championed these injustices.

Institutional stability and social cohesion are important for societies to function well but change is also necessary in order to improve life for everyone. New ideas can arise that challenge the status quo. Christians have always debated whether to adopt, adapt, or abandon these new standards. For instance, should Christians put trees in their homes and decorate them during the winter solstice? Should Christians have bands lead worship services? Should women have leadership roles in church? Is it right to grant divorced people full participation in Christian communities? Should we give gay people full access to church life? These are but a few of thousands of debates Christians have had about what our norms should be. It was only a few decades ago that divorced persons were unwelcome in church and they could not hold leadership positions in most congregations. Today, even evangelical churches readily accept divorced people in church and into leadership positions with little regard for the reason for the divorce.

The main point here is that Christians wrestle with which moral norms must remain and which ones need to be changed. In general, Nurturants are more willing to change some norms. A potential drawback occurs if they change a large number of traditional norms in a short timespan because this can erode trust in institutions. Authoritatives do not want the norms to change because they place a high value on social conformity. The danger here is the tendency to turn a blind eye when societal norms harm particular groups.

WHO IS MY NEIGHBOR?

Surveys show that in America religious people are more civic minded, and volunteer and contribute more to the welfare of their communities.[7] Forty-eight percent of secular people, on the other hand, say that people should take care of themselves. Cain's contemptuous response to God, "Am I my brother's keeper?" does not seem to reflect the attitude of religious Americans. Yet, there is a significant difference between Nurturant and Authoritative religious people when it comes to helping others. The Authoritative types are more parochial in that they tend to help only their in-group rather than outsiders. One's in-group is comprised of like-minded folks such as those who attend the same church, look like them, and share the same values. People with an Authoritative orientation do many wonderful things to help those in their in-group. Those with a Nurturing orientation care for their in-group but also act to help those outside their tribe, including those who look and think differently from them. When it comes to helping people suffering from natural disasters, Nurturants tend to help even if the people are outsiders while Authoritatives are split on the matter. Some Authoritatives believe that the people affected did not deserve their suffering—it is not their fault. However, some Authoritatives believe God punishes people via natural disasters, they deserve to suffer, so we should not help them, especially if they are outsiders.

Some people in Jesus' day wanted to get rid of aliens, particularly Samaritans, in Palestine. They wanted a pure homeland for their Jewish tribe. One such person asked Jesus what it means to live according to God's values. Jesus asks him, what does the Scripture teach? The person says it means to love God and love your neighbor. Jesus says that is correct so live it out. However, the fellow asks for clarification. "Who is my neighbor?" Is my neighbor limited to my in-group of fellow Jews or does it extend beyond my tribe? To answer this question Jesus tells a story called The Good Samaritan (Luke 10). Samaritans were a significant religious minority group in Judaism who lived in a region between Galilee and Judea. Historically, there was a lot of bad blood between Jews and Samaritans. Many Jews thought that touching something owned by a Samaritan made one ritually contaminated which would prevent you from approaching God. In the parable, Jesus says that bandits beat a Jew and left him for dead. Two Jewish religious leaders see the man's condition but refuse to help. However, a

7. Putnam and Campbell, *American Grace*, 444–64.

Samaritan happens by and he transports the injured man to safety and pays for his recovery. The Samaritan cared for someone outside his in-group. In fact, the Samaritan gave his hard-earned cash to help someone who likely despised Samaritans. Jesus teaches that we need to get over our tribalism and stereotypes of other religious groups.

On another occasion, Jesus told a story about appropriate behavior for those who follow God. He says those who feed the hungry, show hospitality to strangers, clothe the naked, heal the sick, and take care of prisoners are the ones who do what God wants done (Matt 25:36–45). He says that doing such things for "the least of these who are members of my family, you did these acts to me." Proponents of the Authoritative view tend to confine "the least members of my family" to members of their tribe while those who affirm Nurturant values believe it means to help anyone in need. Research shows that the instruction to love your neighbor motivates Christians to help others. However, the research also shows that those with Authoritative values tend to help only members of their in-group, while people with Nurturing values care for their in-group as well as for those who are religiously or ethnically different.[8]

COMPARISONS

People who follow the Authoritative way define evil in stark terms and move to stamp it out by any means necessary.[9] They tend to talk about political issues in absolutist terms as a choice between decency and depravity. If you disagree, then you are a degenerate. They are extremely confident in the correctness of their views. On the other hand, those with Nurturant values believe that there is evil but are aware that there are often two sides to a dispute, so one side may not be wholly correct. They have moral convictions yet hold them with humility and are far less willing to demonize those who disagree with them.

A final comparison of these two life orientations concerns how they understand the meaning and value of the Ten Commandments. For the Authoritative way of thinking, the Ten Commandments teach that if you obey God's rules, then you will be successful. These particular commandments have become a powerful symbol standing for the entire Authoritative way of life. In the 1950s plaques of the Ten Commandments were placed in

8. See Shen et al., "Testing," and Blogowska and Saroglou, "Religious."

9. Froese and Bader, *America's Four Gods*, 67, 149, 153.

American public school classrooms and monuments of them were erected on courthouse grounds. For a Nurturing morality, the Ten Commandments disclose how God expects Israel to live now that God has welcomed them to the divine country. Grace is first and it empowers people to transform their lives. Though the Nurturant approach sees the value of the Ten Commandments, the words do not hold the same symbolic value as they do for Authoritatives. Nurturing Christians place a higher value on the Beatitudes of Jesus. Jesus gives the Beatitudes on a mountain, just as Moses received the Ten Commandments on a mountain, and gives a summary of divine expectations for how people should live in God's country (Matt 5). He says God is pleased with the meek, the merciful, and peacemakers. However, Authoritatives are not interested in posting plaques of the Beatitudes in public schools since they think the virtues of the Beatitudes coddle people and do not produce moral strength.

CONCLUSION

The Nurturant and Authoritative styles of Christianity agree on many of the moral maxims that should guide our lives. However, the two approaches produce vastly different moral visions about how to treat people. Generally, the Authoritative view emphasizes individual responsibility while Nurturant values consider both individual responsibility and communitarian concerns important. Authoritatives tend to think of their moral convictions as timeless truths applicable in all times and places. They think their moral stances are correct and so are not open to question. Nurturing folks, on the other hand, readily acknowledge the role of culture in moral reasoning and hold their convictions with humility. They believe they are correct but admit they could need revision. Both approaches believe the social order is important but those who affirm the Authoritative view have a great desire to maintain long-standing social practices and do not tolerate people who challenge them. Those with a Nurturing orientation believe that institutions and traditions may need revision in order to bring them into harmony with God's values. The Nurturant moral vision follows in the footsteps of Jesus.

9

RELIGIOUS POLITICS

The state political convention was a festive and exuberant affair. People energetically waved signs for their candidate or issue. As a delegate, I participated in small groups to build the party platform. During the discussions, I would raise questions about what many of those present took for granted. I was told that if I could not commit myself 100 percent to these ideas, then I did not belong. I was shocked. Later, I helped with the gubernatorial campaign of a colleague. When he lost the election, his wife told me she was upset with God. I thought she was inconsistent since she believed that God decided who got elected and God's decision is best. Because I believe that God does not control elections, I had other explanations for the vote. My colleague who had run for governor suggested, in a friendly way, that I was ill-suited to work in politics.

Chapter 1 discussed the questions regarding traits we prefer in children. The preferences indicate whether someone is Nurturant, Authoritative, or a mix of the two. The responses reveal whether you feel, for instance, the world is a safe or threatening place. The answers accurately predict one's views on issues from income inequality to same-gender marriage.[1] Other research shows that if you tell me what you think God is like, I can tell you your politics.[2] The Nurturant and Authoritative ways of life are motivated by very different core values. Other chapters demonstrate that these values lead to different moral and theological positions. At the heart of our

---

1. See Mockabee, "Question," and Barker and Tinnick, "Competing Visions."
2. See Froese and Bader, *America's Four Gods*.

political divides are the same Nurturant and Authoritative *values*.[3] This does not mean, however, that any political party in any country is wholly Nurturant. In the United States, the Democratic and Republican parties contain both Nurturants and Authoritatives.[4] In addition, biblical writers were well aware that "money talks"—it buys influence and thus the power to get your way. The influence money brings leads many politicians to be more responsive to wealthy constituents and ignore their poor constituents.[5] This chapter is about values rather than party affiliation.

INCOME INEQUALITY

Most people believe that income inequality in America is a significant problem. Over the past forty years, those with incomes in the top fifth saw their incomes increase 68 percent while those in the middle fifth saw an increase of only 23 percent. Those with the lowest wages have fallen way behind. What should we do about this? According to the 2013 Economic Values Survey, 88 percent of religious progressives and 69 percent of religious moderates believe the government should do more to alleviate the imbalance.[6] However, 63 percent of religious conservatives say the government should keep out of this.

The Nurturant and Authoritative values help explain this polarization. Religious Authoritatives believe everyone has adequate opportunities today and blame the poor for not working hard enough. Those from the Nurturant side of the tracks disagree and say that most people are working hard but the laws heavily favor those with the highest incomes. In the latter 1800s the government favored the wealthy over laborers by establishing laws that promoted wealth generated by investments instead of wealth

3. See Lakoff, *Moral Politics*.

4. In 2016 the Democratic Party was around 70 percent Nurturant and the Republican Party was 60 percent Authoritative. See Hetherington and Weiler, *Prius*, 23. For documentation that the Republican Party has become increasingly Authoritative over the past sixty years, see Hetherington and Weiler, *Authoritarianism*.

5. Bartels, *Unequal Democracy*, 238–68. He found that neither Democratic nor Republican senators were responsive to constituents from the bottom third of income. Yet, Democrats did take middle income constituents into account while Republicans were two times more responsive to the wealthy than Democrats.

6. Jones et al., "Do Americans?" Other studies confirm these same findings: Putnam and Campbell, *American Grace*; Froese and Bader, *America's*; and Baylor Religion Survey, "Values and Beliefs."

generated by producing goods or services. Laws changed after the Great Depression to better reward workers for producing things. However, in the 1980s the laws were changed back to resemble those in the nineteenth century. From 1943 to 1973 worker productivity in the USA increased 103 percent and wages went up 103 percent.[7] From 1973 to 2014 net productivity rose 72 percent but wages, after inflation, rose only 8.3 percent for the median worker. Another way to see this is that since 1980, the bottom 90 percent of the workforce has not benefited from the growth—only the top 10 percent has. Working hard no longer guarantees a good income. In fact, the United States is now almost at the bottom of developed countries when it comes to income mobility. In countries such as Canada and Denmark, children have a much better chance of moving into a higher income bracket than their parents compared to the USA. In the 1980s neoliberal philosophy began to spread. According to this approach, individuals, not communities, are the driving force of life. Government services should be privatized. The economy should be a totally "free" market of pure competition, without government regulations. In this way, the market ensures that everyone gets exactly what they deserve.

Neoliberalism fits well with Authoritative values. According to the Authoritative narrative, your economic status is exactly as it should be. If you are well off it is because you worked hard and if you are in financial difficulty it is because you were lazy. For Authoritatives, it is a level playing field. In fact, the government needs to get out of way by removing regulations so the morally strong can succeed. We should cut funding for anti-poverty programs in order to motivate people to work hard. Poverty would be abolished if people simply worked harder. People in many parts of America know they have gotten the economic shaft and are angry. However, they cannot see that their own core values have been used against them, which is why they find scapegoats to blame instead of their Authoritative lawmakers who changed the rules of the economic game.[8]

Those with Nurturing values believe the economic game is unfair because the tax laws favor those from higher income families. The claim that 50 percent of people struggle financially because they do not work hard enough is not credible. In addition, what goes unnoticed is corporate "wealthfare," where wealthy individuals and corporations receive taxpayer

7. Sample, *Working*, 10.

8. Sample's *Working* provides many stories from both urban and rural settings to show this is the case.

funded tax breaks and federal loans at below market rates.[9] It is not a level playing field and the government should adjust the rules. Nurturants see taxes as investments in the community to help it thrive. Quality education and modern infrastructure support the common good to help all of us live out our potential. Responsible economic planning can strengthen communities through stewardship and interdependence. The nation is stronger and more secure when the bulk of the population participates in and benefits from the economy. The nation is like a caravan crossing a desert. The caravan is moving forward but if those at the back fall substantially behind, then the convoy breaks up. It becomes simply dispersed individuals working for their own self-interest rather than a community working together for the common good.[10]

Biblical writers are aware that those with money can use it to exploit others. Deuteronomy says that God shows love to widows, orphans, and aliens by giving them food and clothing (10:18). In biblical times these people were easy pickings for those who wanted to take advantage of them. Proverbs 29:7 says that the righteous care about the rights of the poor while wicked neglect them. James says God is displeased with the rich because they did not pay the laborers their fair wages (5:4). There are hundreds of passages in the Bible against the wealthy using their power to take advantage of others. Some Authoritative believers are aware of these biblical teachings but claim that the way to implement them is for individuals, not the government, to provide charity. Nurturant folks think this is like using a thimble to bail water from the Titanic. Without substantive changes to the economic policies, only those with first-class tickets get lifeboats. The rest drown in the frigid waters, not because they did not swim hard enough, but because the policies of the Titanic decided who lived and who died.

White evangelicals and black Protestants share a great many theological beliefs. For example, they both stress the importance of individual piety, a literal reading of Scripture, and that Jesus is returning soon. Yet, these two groups sharply differ on the role of government and social institutions. Historically, the corporate life of the black church has been far more important to the economic survival of blacks than has church life for whites. Black Christians developed traditions of interdependence on one another

9. See Sample, *Working*, 12–13 and Sides, "How."

10. These comments for how to frame Nurturant values for economic and political issues are found at the website Topos Partnership (www.topospartnership.com) and Lakoff, *Don't Think.*

leading to strong communitarian impulses. Black Christians, as opposed to white evangelicals, believe that institutions such as government should take a prominent role in areas such as alleviating income inequality and providing health care.

The majority of white evangelicals, on the other hand, place a high priority on individualism—taking responsibility for your own life. This leads them to believe that government should only provide freedom from regulations because this allows people to either develop the moral strength to succeed, or become weak and fail. They criticize black Christians for relying on social programs instead of individual effort and for blaming institutions instead of themselves for their situation. They say the economic divide between whites and blacks would disappear if blacks only worked harder because the system is fair and each individual gets what he or she deserves.[11] In fact, many white Christians say that though blacks may be Christians, they are not true *American* Christians because they do not fully practice Authoritative religion.[12]

Authoritatives believe the wealthy are the "good" people in society because their wealth is the product of individual hard work by people who played by the rules. Hence, government should not "punish" the "best" people with higher taxes. Doing so would take the hard-earned money of the good and give it to non-producing welfare queens who want something for nothing and do not take responsibility for their lives. Those with Authoritative values feel disgust towards "free riders" who get something for nothing. They are "parasites" rather than producers. That is why Jerry Falwell Junior can say it is just common sense that a poor person has never contributed anything of value to society.[13] If you do not contribute, then you do not deserve anything. Authoritatives subscribe to the "dependency thesis," which asserts that people become dependent on others when they are given help instead of being forced to do it themselves.

Those with Nurturing values acknowledge that some people abuse both the generosity of God and government programs. However, they believe that God gives divine gifts in order to empower people to change even though God is aware that some will abuse the gifts. Most people work hard to support themselves and their families but sometimes need help. But current economic policies and structures do not automatically

11. See Hetherington and Weiler, *Prius*, 45, 168.
12. See Emerson et al., "Equal in Christ."
13. Heim, "Jerry Falwell Jr."

reward those who work hard. You can swim vigorously against a strong current but you may not get anywhere. Those born with motorboats have a definite advantage.

The Greek and Roman philosophers taught that mercy was a character defect. Giving someone what they did not deserve was immoral. In the second and third centuries, Christian pastors regularly went against this accepted morality. They praised those who gave money or gifts to people who could offer nothing in return because it imitated the magnanimous grace of God. In the Roman world, giving things to others was a highly calculated affair. The wealthy gave only if they received something of significance in return. Roman society said to help those who could help you. However, Jesus said to give to anyone who asks and expect nothing in return (Luke 6:30, 35). He said to follow the example of God's compassion (Luke 6:36), which gives indiscriminately to those who cannot reciprocate. Jesus and the New Testament writers reject the Roman calculating and discriminating approach to giving.[14]

Jesus lavished grace on those who had not deserved it. He healed the sick without worrying whether this would make them dependent. He freely gave acceptance to those who did not deserve it. We all benefit from things we did not earn. For example, we have communities with roads and utilities, a language, educational systems, and farmers who supply food. God created a world with gifts we did not deserve. The idea that everyone receives exactly what they deserve is ludicrous. Of course, people need to work hard and contribute to the community, but simply giving everyone what they deserve is not the Christian way. At one point Jesus told a parable to explain what living in God's country is like (Matt 20). He says the owner of a vineyard hired workers early in the morning and agreed to pay them $150 for the day. Then at noon, he hired more workers and in the late afternoon, he hired even more. When it came time to pay the workers he gave those who only worked an hour and those who worked the entire day the same $150. At this, those who had worked all day grumbled saying the others did not deserve as much as they did. The owner replied that it was virtuous to be ridiculously generous to those who did not deserve it. This is how God treats us.

To the Authoritative mindset, this is no way to run a business or a country. Such financial extravagance will ruin it. It is morally superior to believe that God gives people precisely what they deserve. If people work

14. See Jipp, *Saved By*, 157–68.

hard and follow the rules, then they will be financially prosperous. If they do not, then God will punish them with economic hardship. Surveys show that "Americans with the lowest incomes have the angriest and most judgmental Gods."[15] They believe God is angry at the poor and loves the wealthy. Jesus, however, rejected these ideas. He said it is easier for a camel to go through the eye of a needle than for a rich person to enter God's kingdom (Matt 19:24). Upon hearing this, the disciples were "perplexed" because they believed that being wealthy was proof that God had blessed you.

RACE

In 2011, the median household income for a white family was $67,000, $40,000 for Latino and black families, and $35,000 for Native American families. There is also a huge wealth gap. In 2013, the net worth of white households was $141,900, versus $13,700 for Latinos and $11,000 for blacks.[16] Do whites simply work harder than everyone else? Or, have the laws privileged whites in our history?

White Authoritatives say they are not racist and by their own definition they are not. They define racism as people who hate Blacks or use the "N" word.[17] This definition ignores three problems. First, cognitive science shows that all people have implicit bias. We are not aware that our minds give favorable and unfavorable assessments of others. Researchers developed an Implicit Bias Association Test and found that most Americans have an unconscious preference for whites over blacks. Second, many whites believe the Authoritative narrative that the sole reason they are better off is due to their own individual effort. We are solely responsible for our fates. It has nothing to do with attending better quality schools that received more tax dollars or that for generations, local, state, and federal government policies along with businesses and banks discriminated against minorities. For example, after World War II, white soldiers received funding for job training or to attend college. They were given loan guarantees to purchase their first house. Significantly less money was given to African American veterans. They were directed into training programs for low-paying jobs, denied admission to many colleges, and were turned down for home and business

15. Froese and Bader, *America's*, 114.

16. Wallis, *America's Original Sin*, 40 and 43.

17. The information in this section is indebted to Wallis, *America's Original Sin*, 73–96 and Sample, *Working Class Rage*, 61–85.

loans. Many cities had "red line" laws that required blacks to live in specified areas and prohibited whites from selling their homes to blacks. Legal documents called blacks an "invasive species" in order to exclude them from government-subsidized suburban developments. This meant that when housing values rose significantly in the next several decades, only whites benefited. The increase in wealth allowed white children to receive better educations and their social networks allowed for better job opportunities for their children and grandchildren. In short, the policies of governments, businesses, and banks resulted in affirmative action for whites.

The third problem with defining racism as overt hatred of minorities is that racism is subtle and changes form over time. Legendary political strategist Lee Atwater explained that in the 1950s you could be racist and use the N word but that changed in the late 1960s. They had to disguise their racism by talking about forced busing and States rights. In 1980 they figured out how to implement racism with tax cuts. Atwater explained, "You're talking about cutting taxes . . . and a byproduct of them is, blacks get hurt worse than whites . . . 'We want to cut this,' is more abstract than even the busing thing, uh, and a hell of lot more abstract than the N-word . . ."[18] Racism can take many forms and disguises and can even seem legitimate by saying that the recipients of government programs are undeserving.

Nurturants affirm the need to work hard and take personal responsibility for one's life. Yet, there are also systems, such as education and banking, that play a role in our fate and sometimes these systems were designed to favor one group at the expense of another. The Authoritative tale that it is never legitimate to blame the systems—just blame yourself—is false. Our lives involve a mix of both personal responsibility and systems, which is why we need to encourage individuals to work hard and establish laws to ensure that our economic, educational, and other systems, give everyone an opportunity to reach their potential.

Another topic in religious politics related to race is the development of the Religious Right. According to Paul Weyrich, Ed Dobson, Grover Norquist, and others who founded this movement, what galvanized evangelicals and fundamentalists to form a political movement was the 1970 Internal Revenue Service's (IRS) decision to revoke the tax exempt status of private white-only K-12 academies and colleges.[19] Without the subsidy of

18. Cited in Hetherington and Weiler, *Prius*, 58.

19. For documentation see Balmer, *Evangelicalism*, 109–21 and Prothero, *Why*, 187–90.

tax dollars, these schools could not survive. They felt this threatened their evangelical-fundamentalist subculture. The Religious Right began on this racial issue, not abortion. At first, a number of leading evangelicals affirmed the *Roe v. Wade* decision and the Religious Right did not oppose abortion for many years.[20]

HEALTH CARE

In America, millions of people have no health insurance and even those who do struggle to afford the co-pays and deductibles for the prescription drugs and procedures they need. Many people have to choose whether to purchase their medicine or buy food. Americans are now $88 billion in debt for health care. What should we do?

For Authoritatives, health care is best understood as a business that produces a commodity. Commodities are things like cars and TVs. Some people can afford a good quality car and good quality health care. People should work hard to get a job that provides good health insurance and pays enough money for the deductibles. As one person told me, "If they can't make it, let them die." Not every Authoritative will embrace this conclusion but it fits the mindset of giving people only what they deserve.

Nurturants see health care as part of the common good. Just like good roads and schools, healthy people contribute to the flourishing of the community. It was a huge mistake for President Obama to call the program the Affordable Care Act because the word "affordable" prompts the idea that health care is a commodity—the way Authoritatives view it. In addition, affordability can imply cheap. Health care can be framed differently. One way to think of it is freedom. Freedom from illness. Freedom from economic devastation. The freedom to change jobs or start a business and still have access to health care. In addition, people without good quality health insurance are more prone to infection and disease that can spread to others. This way of framing health care helps persuade Authoritatives. They tend to fear contamination so it makes sense to them that providing everyone with good health care produces a healthier and safer society for all. The vast majority of religious progressives and moderates say the government should guarantee health care for all citizens while 74 percent of conservatives disagree.[21]

20. See Balmer, *Evangelicalism*, 109–15 and Prothero, *Why*, 185–87.

21. Jones et al., "Do Americans?"

CRIMINAL JUSTICE

Those who believe in a judgmental and Authoritative God believe that those who violate social and religious norms deserve harsh punishment.[22] Those with an angry and judgmental God believe that criminals deserve lengthy sentences and the death penalty.[23] The discussions in chapter 5 regarding how different understandings of justice led to different views of atonement and redemption come into play here as well. Authoritatives value law and order and believe that God is tough on sin so we have to be tough on crime. Violating the law creates guilt and justice requires punishment. Retributive justice demands that violators get what they deserve.

Those who believe in a benevolent God tend to see crime as a violation of people and obligations towards them.[24] Violations create an obligation to restore and heal the situation. Justice involves the entire community, including the victim and the offender, to put things right. Restorative justice concentrates on the needs of the victim and the responsibility of the offender to repair the harm. Nurturant values motivate a need to rehabilitate offenders rather than simply locking them up in a brutalizing environment.

In addition, the two models help explain the very different responses to the highly publicized police shootings of minority people. Here is Franklin Graham's solution to the problem. "Listen up—Blacks, Whites, Latinos, and everybody else. Most police shootings can be avoided. It comes down to respect for authority and obedience. If a police officer tells you to stop, you stop. . . . YOU OBEY. Parents, teach your children to respect and obey those in authority."[25] Other evangelical leaders wrote a letter in response saying that Graham's solution was simplistic, ignored the testimonies of minorities, and disregarded the "legal regimes that enslaved and oppressed people of color, made in the image of God—from Native American genocide and containment, to colonial and antebellum slavery, through Jim Crow and peonage, to our current system of mass incarceration and criminalization."[26] Once again, Authoritatives say the problem is solved solely by individual obedience and ignore unjust systems.[27]

22. Froese and Bader, "God in America," 475.

23. Bader et al., "Divine Justice."

24. For a summary of these two approaches, see Wallis, *America's Original Sin*, 165.

25. Cited in Wallis, *America's Original Sin*, 52–53.

26. Cited in Wallis, *America's Original Sin*, 54.

27. In 2015 the President's Task Force on 21st Century Policing made a number of suggestions. See President's Task Force.

SAME-GENDER MARRIAGE

Marriage confers legal and social status so it is an important institution. Nurturants tend to define marriage in terms of love and commitment. It involves the sanctity of two people publicly making a life commitment to one another. They take responsibility for caring for one another. Many conclude that committed couples should have the freedom to marry the person they love regardless of gender. Authoritatives, on the other hand, defined marriage as a union of a man and a woman. During the public debate they highlighted the issue of gender instead of love, responsibility, and commitment. The debate in religious communities over how to treat LGBTQ people and what to do about gay marriage has been enormous. Denominations have split over the issue and large numbers of millennials have left the church because of negative treatment of LGBTQ people.[28]

Religious Authoritatives oppose gay marriage for several reasons. One is the claim that the Bible says same-gender sexual relationships are immoral. Another reason is the claim that same-gender marriage violates traditional social norms. Because Authoritatives prefer conformity to change (see chapter 8) they feel that changes to traditional ways of treating people indicates decay in society. That is why gay marriage has become the flag around which Authoritatives rally—it symbolizes the loss of traditional Authoritative morals.

Many religious Nurturants use the Bible to support acceptance of same-gender relations. Some argue that the seven biblical texts cited by Authoritatives have been misinterpreted. These texts are not about what we today refer to as same-gender relationships or being gay. Rather, the cultural context shows that some of these biblical texts are about immoral demonstrations of power over others (such as male and female rape) while others address practices done in the worship of idols.[29] Others hold that even if these biblical texts do actually condemn what we today call same-gender relationships, that does not necessarily mean the conversation is over. After all, some biblical texts affirm slavery and beating your children with rods, but we no longer believe these are moral or loving. There are texts in the Bible that guide us to set aside other texts in the Bible (see chapter 6) and the biblical teaching on loving others directs Christians to

28. Public Religion Research Institute, "Survey."

29. For a survey of how these biblical texts are interpreted, see Gushee, *Changing*. For a careful study that tries not to claim more than the evidence allows, see Gnuse, "Seven Gay Texts."

grant full participation to LGBTQ people. In addition, though Nurturants value traditions, they are more open to changes in societal norms when they believe the norms are harming particular groups (see chapter 8).

DEMOCRACY

Democracies around the world have been hard hit in the last decade due to the worldwide resurgence of Authoritative values.[30] Even in the United States, key characteristics of democracy are threatened. In 2017, researchers asked Americans about some important characteristics of democracies.[31] Here are three of the questions they asked. (1) Whether it is important for a democracy to protect the rights of those with unpopular views. Seventy percent of Nurturants said it was very important while only a third of Authoritatives agreed. (2) Should democracies protect the rights of news organizations to criticize political leaders? Three-quarters of Nurturants said it is important while only a quarter of Authoritatives did. (3) Should people have the right of nonviolent protest? While 78 percent of Nurturants believe it is very important, only half of Authoritatives thought so. The researchers also asked whether it was a good idea to have "a strong leader who does not have to bother with Congress or elections." Around 70 percent of Nurturants said this is a "very bad" idea while only a third of Authoritatives thought it harmful. Authoritatives prefer autocratic leaders who "have extreme confidence in their own abilities and make independent decisions without the input of others."[32]

The differences between autocratic leaders and those with Nurturant values is brought out in Christian works such as C. S. Lewis's *The Lion, The Witch, and the Wardrobe* and *That Hideous Strength*, and J. R. R. Tolkien's *Lord of the Rings*. The same traits are portrayed as well in the *Star Wars* and *Harry Potter* series. In these stories, autocratic rulers desire subservience and obedience and use fear and intimidation to get their way. They ask others to sacrifice for them. Nurturant rulers desire community grounded in love and empathy. They often sacrifice themselves for others. Another feature in these works is that Nurturants include a wide array of diverse types of beings and races in their communities and value their input while Authoritatives do this much less, if at all.

30. See Hetherington and Weiler, *Prius*, 190–214.

31. Hetherington and Weiler, *Prius*, 187–88.

32. Gelfand et al., "Trump."

Nurturants are the ones in various countries working to establish or uphold democracy along with freedom of expression, religious freedom, and participation of all in society. In churches and other institutions, this way of life fosters respect for others and a desire for all people to have a voice in the public square. A key issue is who gets to participate in a community or democracy. Chapter 6 discussed the incredibly contentious issue that threatened to divide the early Jesus community—whether to grant Gentiles full participation in the church without them first becoming Jewish. They made the history-changing decision to be inclusive and multiracial. Yet, Christian communities have struggled to continue this trajectory by allowing women and others to fully participate. Similarly, Americans have repeatedly wrestled over who gets to participate in the democratic process. Authoritatives seek to restrict who is part of the American family and put laws in place to limit the voices of women and minorities. Nurturants, on the other hand, have worked for a more expansive understanding of who is included in the American family and to expand participation of more groups in the life of the nation. The so called "culture wars" have been a repeated debate over who counts as a "true" American.[33]

Some people refer to the two models as "tight and loose" cultures and the differences between them sum up much of our discussion so far. A team of researchers studied thirty-three nations along with the fifty United States.[34] They found that prototypically "tight" societies had the strictest laws, harshest punishments, and low tolerance for dissenters. They tend to use corporal punishment in schools and favor the death penalty. Tighter states, such as Alabama and Mississippi, have the highest death rates from natural disasters and have high rates of infectious diseases compared to looser states.[35] People in tighter societies prefer autocratic leaders who control the government without checks and balances on their power. "Loose" societies, by contrast, have few rigidly enforced rules, work for rehabilitation of offenders, have greater tolerance for differences between people, prefer democracies, and promote empathy and dialogue. Some researchers refer to the values undergirding democracy worldwide as "emancipative values."[36]

---

33. For an insightful history of the culture wars, see Prothero, *Why*.

34. Gelfand et al., "Differences." See also, Aktas et al., "Cultural Tightness-Looseness."

35. In addition, areas with high concentrations of Authoritative religion produce higher divorce rates. See Glass and Levchak, "Red."

36. See Welzel and Inglehart, "Political Culture" and "Cultural Map."

These values give priority to gender equality over patriarchy, tolerance over conformity, autonomy over authority, and participation over security.

Nurturant values support key democratic principles such as welcoming others to the public square, freedom of the press, separation of powers, the right to nonviolent protest, and the rejection of authoritarian rulers.

EVANGELICALS AND TRUMP

In the 2016 election, 81 percent of evangelicals voted for Trump—a much higher percentage than voted for Bush, McCain, or Romney in earlier elections. Despite his sexual immorality and habitual lying, which go against Authoritative values, they vigorously support him. They take any criticism of Trump as criticism of God because God chose him to be president. Jerry Falwell Jr. says that "he can't imagine Trump doing anything that's not good for the country."[37] Some of my evangelical friends feel betrayed and express incredulity at this. However, I think it makes sense because research shows that far and away the best predictor of support for Trump is the degree to which one affirms Authoritative values.[38]

Authoritatives tend to believe their views are absolutely correct, see no need for nuance or qualification, and do not practice perspective-taking (see chapter 7). They like leaders who manifest extreme confidence in their own judgment and make decisions without input from others. On the campaign trail, Trump said he knew more than all the generals and experts and repeatedly claimed that only he could fix America's problems. Whereas George W. Bush worked to create an international coalition regarding Iraq, Trump prefers to go it alone. Authoritatives practice the reciprocity principle: if someone does good to you, then you do something good for them, and if they harm you, then you harm them. This fits with Trump's favorite Bible verse: "an eye for an eye."[39] There is no grace here (see chapters 2 and 5). Authoritatives focus on their own in-group and are fearful of those who do not look and believe as they do. Members of other tribes such as minorities, immigrants, and, in particular, Muslims, are threats to their tribe.

The Authoritative playbook predated Trump and he learned it well. A repeated narrative of white religious Authoritatives, from the Puritans to

---

37. Heim, "Jerry."
38. Taub, "Rise," and Gelfand et al., "Trump."
39. Fea, *Believe*, 3.

today, is that the country is going downhill and away from God.[40] In times past, evangelicals railed against Catholic immigration, claimed the federal government was going to take away their Bibles, and southern evangelicals feared the end of slave labor. Today, Authoritatives rail against non-white immigration, worry that the government will take away their guns, and feel their subculture is under attack with the loss of federal subsidies for their segregated academies and the legalization of same-gender marriage. In *Believe Me: the Evangelical Road to Donald Trump*, historian John Fea says the playbook for getting evangelicals to vote for you involves fear, power, and nostalgia.[41] You appeal to white evangelical fear that the broader culture is moving away from them. Then you promise to give them the political power to enforce their values on society. Finally, you stoke the longing for a mythologized past—when America was a Christian nation run by white Christian males. Trump followed the playbook by speaking of "enemies" destroying our values and promising power to evangelicals to restore America to a past greatness.

Religious Authoritatives rally behind what they define as "strong" leaders and obey them. In addition, when they feel threatened, they aggressively react to outsiders. Above, it was noted that Authoritatives tend to say that leaders should not be criticized. Of course, professional journalists regularly raise questions and in response Trump calls them "enemies" and "scum." Many evangelicals love when Trump calls political opponents names even when the target is a teenage female. Some evangelicals justify this by saying that Jesus called some of the religious leaders of his day names. But mostly, they feel that Trump is their champion in slaying the enemies of Authoritative morals. One might think that evangelicals would prefer someone like Vice President Pence. However, a number of evangelicals say Pence is too soft to get the job done.[42] They prefer a leader who makes those opposed to Authoritative values submit to his will. Some justify this by saying they are not electing a pastor to be President. Trump is their protector like the Persian king Cyrus. Just as Cyrus allowed the Jews to return to their homeland, Trump is allowing evangelicals to return to their mythic lost country.

Many evangelicals hold that God chooses our political leaders according to the Bible (Dan 2), so if you have a problem with them, then you

40. See Fea, *Believe*, and Prothero, *Why*.

41. This playbook works for Authoritatives in other religions as well such as with Modi in India and Erdoğan in Turkey.

42. Bruenig, "In God's."

should take it up with God. God put them in authority and they should not be criticized. Authoritatives think that protesting laws and criticizing leaders undermines respect for authority.[43] Tauren Wells, a popular Christian singer, sums this up nicely: "I would never oppose a president because I believe in what Scripture says about giving honor to authority. That doesn't mean that I agree with everything. But I believe that an attack on authority anywhere is an attack on authority everywhere."[44] The ideas of God choosing political leaders and that we should not criticize leaders fits with Authoritative values. However, I do not believe Authoritative evangelicals consistently practice these beliefs. I never heard an evangelical Authoritative say that if you had a problem with President Obama, then you should take it up with God. Moreover, evangelicals criticized Obama mercilessly for pretty much everything he did from his reversal of support for the Defense of Marriage Act to the way he saluted a Marine.

In December of 2019, *Christianity Today*, the leading magazine for evangelical Christianity, published the editorial "Trump Should Be Removed from Office." It called Trump a "grossly immoral character" who has abused his power and so is unfit to be president. The editor then quoted what the magazine said about President Bill Clinton twenty years previously and said they stand on the same principles now as they did when they supported the impeachment of Clinton. "That he [Trump] should be removed, we believe, is not a matter of partisan loyalties but loyalty to the Creator of the Ten Commandments." It says that the uncritical support of Trump is damaging the Christian witness: "will anyone take anything we say about justice and righteousness with any seriousness for decades to come?"[45] Though the editorial uses a number of Authoritative values to make its case, a few days later, around 200 evangelical leaders published a scathing response to the magazine for criticizing both the President and those who support him. I applaud *Christianity Today* for attempting to open a conversation within the evangelical community about its support of Trump. Yet, just as I was told that I did not belong because I asked questions, so they were told there was no need for a conversation. The evangelical leaders already have their protector and no questioning is allowed if you

43. There are "Aggressive Authoritatives" who do protest against elected officials. They believe that the only legitimate authorities are those who affirm Authoritative values. They want total control of government, exclusion of other views, and harsh punishments for those who disagree. See Jacobs, "Inside the Minds."

44. Blake, "Why."

45. Galli, "Trump Should Be Removed from Office."

want to remain in the tribe. God put Trump in office so who do you think you are to question God?

CONCLUSION

The core values of Nurturants and Authoritatives lead them to very different stances on religion and politics. Nurturants prize interdependence and see the need for both personal responsibility and fair systems so that all have the opportunity to develop their full potential. Authoritatives highlight individual responsibility and downplay systems. They believe everyone gets what they deserve because it is a level playing field.

Authoritatives want to return to a past when, they believe, things were much better. Of course, that past was not better for blacks, Native Americans, and women. Nurturants identify good values in the American past such as the Constitution and Bill of Rights but think that we still have work to do so that everyone benefits from them. Nurturants tend to look forward to an improved America rather than backwards to a mythological past. They have hope for the future that love will drive out fear. They highlight grace over law, emancipative values, and seek to follow a loving and merciful God who gives people what they do not deserve.

Authoritatives refer to their political opponents as "enemies" with whom they are at "war" for the culture. The point of war is to kill and subdue your enemies, so politics has become a blood sport for many religious Authoritatives. In politics, there can be no compromise and so there is no need for dialogue.[46] Nurturants believe we are on a journey together and we sometimes disagree about the best route to take toward our destination. When we disagree, we do not kill our fellow travelers. Rather, we use perspective-taking to understand them and dialogue to persuade them. The metaphors—warfare or journey—shape the way we treat one another, so we need to watch what we say.

Finally, evangelical and political Authoritatives have joined together. In 1981, Billy Graham had a conversation with Jerry Falwell and then expressed a worry he had about the Religious Right. "I don't want to see religious bigotry in any form. It would disturb me if there was a wedding between the religious fundamentalists and the political right. The hard right

---

46. A number of the far left also shut down dialogue if you do not agree completely with them. In addition, the call-out culture that excludes forgiveness and makes no attempt at rehabilitation has no grace.

has no interest in religion except to manipulate it."[47] Graham feared a marriage between evangelicals/fundamentalists and the political right. What he did not understand is that it was a match made in Authoritative heaven.

47. Graham, "Interview."

10

HOMECOMING

When surveys ask people their religious affiliation, some check the box "none." In 1991, only 6 percent of Americans were religiously unaffiliated. Today, 25 percent are unaffiliated. The fastest growth category in American religion is the "nones," with a staggering 39 percent of people ages eighteen to twenty-nine claiming this identification.[1] Many nones remain quite interested in spirituality but do not find organized religion appealing. A five-year study looked at people who had been active in church during their teens but then had a prolonged disconnection or permanently left.[2] A shocking 59 percent of people aged eighteen to twenty-nine have left the church for an extended period or permanently. There is no single reason for these changes. Yet, a significant number of those interviewed mention several reasons. One is that they see the church as close-minded. They describe their experience as "stifling, fear-based and risk-averse." They lament that church is not a safe place for them to ask questions or express doubts. Those in charge claim to know all the answers and do not allow anyone to question the accepted position. Others said, "Christians demonize everything outside the church." As a result, the "church is like a country club, only for insiders." In particular, they say that congregations tend to be "afraid of the beliefs of other faiths." Another reason is that they experienced a focus on rules—obedience was more important than people were. Others said that negative teachings about gays was the reason they left. Some equated Christianity with evangelicalism and the conservative

1. See Cooper et al., "Exodus."
2. See Barna Research Group, "Six Reasons."

political views evangelicals champion.[3] Many young people say that if being religious means affirming Authoritative politics, then religion is not for them. A common theme among these responses is the rejection of Authoritative values. If being religious means one has to affirm the Authoritative way of life, then they want no part of it.

Jesus taught the Nurturing way of life and sought to get those who follow the Authoritative way to turn around and follow him. He said that this would pit family members against one another (Matt 10:34–39). Religious Nurturants and Authoritatives clashed in the first century and in every century since. Today, we feel the polarization in society and the split in families. We need congregations and networks that practice the Nurturing gospel of Jesus in order to reach these people. This book provides support from the teachings of Jesus and the Bible that God engages us in Nurturing ways. The discussions in this book on how to understand God, grace, salvation, the Bible, styles of relating, and politics, show what authentic Christianity looks like.

Some might suggest that we need to combine the Nurturant and Authoritative approaches to find a middle ground. This would be a mistake. The Introduction and chapter 2 discussed three parenting styles that differ according to the degree to which parents are responsive and emotionally warm, on the one hand, and express high expectations, on the other. The two polar views are the Permissive and the Authoritative. The Permissive type accepts whatever the child does and expects little while the Authoritative parent is low in terms of acceptance and high on demanding obedience to the rules. The middle position is the Nurturing parent who has the optimal mix of responsiveness and expectations.

This book showed that the Nurturing way of life is what Jesus taught and is the overarching depiction of what God is like in the Bible. It also showed that Nurturant values help people thrive in all areas of life. Numerous studies demonstrate that a Nurturing way of life produces people who are more self-reliant, confident, prosocial, motivated, and cheerful. We also saw that believing in a Nurturing deity fosters more accepting and forgiving people. Those with a Nurturing life orientation have better mental and spiritual health as well as more trusting and secure relationships. Questions do not threaten them because they acknowledge that we only know in part. Nurturants allow for a constrained pluralism on many doctrines and so are not fearful of Christians with different views. They see the Christian life as

3. Putnam and Campbell, *American Grace*, 3.

a pilgrimage and expect things to change. Nurturants value empathy and democratic concerns to ensure that all people have a voice in what happens. They seek to practice "love your neighbor" in the way of the Good Samaritan by helping both insiders and outsiders. Nurturing values focus on interdependence and the common good in order to produce educational, economic, and other systems that enable each person to achieve their potential. The Nurturing way of life produces better people, better congregations, and better societies.

This contrasts sharply with harmful Authoritative religion that is fear-based, exclusionary, intolerant, untrusting, anxiety-ridden, and allows only one view on any topic. It fosters authoritarian leadership rather than democracy. It demands conformity and punishes those who cross boundaries. It distorts divine love into "If you obey me, then I will love you." It perverts divine justice and twists the good news of Jesus into a moral accounting scheme directed by a very strict judge. It rejects Jesus' teaching about doing good to those who harm you and forgiving others. Hence, it is not surprising that Authoritative thinkers develop doctrines such as penal substitution and hell as an eternal torture chamber, and champion political policies that favor a few individuals over the common good. They do not worship the God Jesus revealed.

Fortunately, our neural circuitry is malleable, so those who follow the Authoritative way can change. Our view of God can change as we learn God's liberating story, encounter changing life situations, and associate with Nurturant people.[4] Thus, if you wish to become more thoroughly Nurturing in your Christian walk, it is important to find like-minded people to assist you. Many books, websites, podcasts, and blogs support a Nurturing way of life. There are many Catholics and Protestants articulating Nurturing Christianity, including Richard Rohr, Rachel Held Evans, Jen Hatmaker, Brian McLaren, Rob Bell, Phyllis Tickle, and N. T. Wright, to name but a few. Though they may not use the terms, Nurturant and Authoritative, these categories nicely sum up what these writers stand for and what they oppose.

Social scientists use the two cognitive models, Nurturant and Authoritative, to describe two alternative moral visions or sets of values. The models help explain why people tend to vote the way they do and the stance they take on social issues. They also help us understand the increasing polarization we feel. I believe these same cognitive models have tremendous

4. Johnson et al., "Mind of the Lord."

explanatory power for helping Christians understand why they disagree on so many doctrines and moral issues. The core values affirmed by each type lead to very different understandings of God, sin, salvation, the nature of the Christian life, the role of Scripture, our cognitive style, and whether to help outsiders.

Those with a Nurturing orientation need to become more aware of these values and regularly state them publicly so that our communities clearly understand what we stand for. Over the past forty years, Authoritative believers have been much better at highlighting their core values, repeating them in public, and applying them to social issues and public policies. They created organizations and think tanks to trumpet their core values and shape society. Those who affirm the Nurturant way of life need to do the same because this way of life produces healthy churches and societies. We need to imitate God's Nurturing values and be able to explain to others the values behind the stances we take on social issues.

The book began with the parable of the Prodigal Son and his homecoming. The son who had turned away from his family decides to return home, but as a hired hand rather than a son. However, the father will have none of it and demonstrates his acceptance of his "lost" son by running to meet him, hugging him, and celebrating his return with a party. Of course, most of us have not done what the prodigal son did. Yet, the story furnishes us with crucial insights about God. God lavishes grace on wayward children in the hopes of winning them back and changing their lives. Welcoming prodigals and following the Nurturant way of life is, as Paul says, "a more excellent way" (1 Cor 12:31).

BIBLIOGRAPHY

Abar, Beau, et al. "The Effects of Maternal Parenting Style and Religious Commitment on Self-Regulation, Academic Achievement, and Risk Behavior among African American Parochial College Students." *Journal of Adolescence* 32 (2009) 259–73.

Aktas, Mert, et al. "Cultural Tightness-Looseness and Perceptions of Effective Leadership." *Journal of Cross-Cultural Psychology* 47.2 (2016) 294–309.

Anselm. *Why God Became Man*. In *St. Anselm: Basic Writings*. Translated by S. N. Deane. La Salle, IL: Open Court, 1962.

Bader, Christopher, and Paul Froese. "Images of God: The Effect of Personal Theologies on Moral Attitudes, Political Affiliation, and Religious Behavior." *Interdisciplinary Journal of Research on Religion* 1 (2005) 2–24.

———. "Unraveling Religious Worldviews: The Relationship Between Images of God and Political Ideology in a Cross-Cultural Analysis." *The Sociological Quarterly* 49 (2008) 689–718.

Bader, Christopher, et al. "Divine Justice: The Relationship Between Images of God and Attitudes Toward Criminal Punishment." *Criminal Justice Review* 35.1 (2010) 90–106.

Baker, Sharon. *Razing Hell: Rethinking Everything You've Been Taught about God's Wrath and Judgement*. Louisville: Westminster John Knox, 2010.

Balmer, Randall. *Evangelicalism in America*. Waco, TX: Baylor University Press, 2016.

Barker, David, and James Tinnick. "Competing Visions of Parental Roles and Ideological Constraint." *American Political Science Review* 100.2 (2006) 249–69.

Barna Research Group. "Six Reasons Young People Leave Church." 2011. https://www.barna.com/research/six-reasons-young-christians-leave-church/.

Bartels, Larry. *Unequal Democracy: The Political Economy of the New Gilded Age*. 2d ed. Princeton: Princeton University Press, 2018.

Baumrind, Dianna. "The Influence of Parenting Style on Adolescent Competence and Substance Abuse." *Journal of Early Adolescence* 11 (1991) 56–95.

Baylor Religion Survey Wave 5. "American Values, Mental Health, and Using Technology in the Age of Trump." September 2017.

Baylor Religion Survey Wave 3. "The Values and Beliefs of the American Public." September 2011.

Beck, Richard. "Defensive Versus Existential Religion: Is Religious Defensiveness Predictive of Worldview Defense?" *Journal of Psychology and Theology* 34.2 (2006) 143–53.

———. "God as Secure Base: Attachment to God and Theological Exploration." *Journal of Psychology and Theology* 34.2 (2006) 125–32.

Benson, Peter, and Bernard Spilka. "God Image as a Function of Self-Esteem and Locus of Control." *Journal for the Scientific Study of Religion* 12 (1973) 297–310.

Blake, John. "Why Christian Music's Biggest Stars Refuse to Change Their Tune for the Trump Era." CNN, October 15, 2019.

Blogowska, Joanna, and Vassilis Saroglou. "Religious Fundamentalism and Limited Proscociality as a Function of the Target." *Journal for the Scientific Study of Religion* 50.1 (2011) 44–60.

Boyd, Gregory. *Cross Vision: How the Crucifixion of Jesus Makes Sense of Old Testament Violence.* Minneapolis: Fortress, 2017.

Bradshaw, Matt, et al., "Attachment to God, Images of God, and Psychological Distress in a Nationwide Sample of Presbyterians." *International Journal for the Psychology of Religion* 20 (2010) 130–47.

———. "Prayer, God Imagery, and Symptoms of Psychopathology." *Journal for the Scientific Study of Religion* 47.4 (2008) 644–59.

Brokaw, Beth, and Keith Edwards. "The Relationship of God Image to Level of Object Relations Development." *Journal of Psychology and Theology* 22.4 (1994) 352–71.

Bruenig, Elizabeth. "In God's Country: Evangelicals View Trump as Their Protector. Will They Stand by Him in 2020?" *Washington Post*, August, 14, 2019.

Bun, John, et al. "Effects of Parental Authoritarianism and Authoritativeness on Self-Esteem." *Personality and Social Psychology Bulletin* 14 (1988) 271–82.

Buri, John, and Rebecca Mueller. "Psychoanalytic Theory and Loving God Concepts." *Journal of Psychology* 127.1 (1993) 17–27.

Bushman, Brad, et al. "When God Sanctions Killing: Effect of Scriptural Violence on Aggression." *Psychological Science* 18.3 (2007) 204–7.

Bynum, Caroline Walker. *Jesus as Mother: Studies in the Spirituality of the High Middle Ages.* Berkeley, CA: University of California Press, 1982.

Carpenter, C. C. J., et al. "A Call for Unity." 1963. https://www.whatsoproudlywehail.org/curriculum/the-american-calendar/a-call-for-unity.

Colijn, Brenda. *Images of Salvation in the New Testament.* Downers Grove, IL: InterVarsity, 2010.

Cooper, Betsy, et al. "Exodus: Why Americans are Leaving Religion—and Why They're Unlikely to Come Back." 2016. https://www.prri.org/research/prri-rns-poll-nones-atheist-leaving-religion/.

Corey, Benjamin. *Unafraid: Moving Beyond Fear-Based Faith.* New York: HarperOne, 2017.

Edwards, Jonathan. "Sinners in the Hands of an Angry God." In *Jonathan Edwards: Basic Writings*, edited by Ola Winslow, 150–67. New York: New American Library, 1966.

Emerson, Michael, et al. "Equal in Christ, but Not in the World: White Conservative Protestants and Explanations of Black-White Inequality." *Social Problems* 46.3 (August 1999) 398–417.

Enns, Peter. *Incarnation and Inspiration: Evangelicals and the Problem of the Old Testament.* 2d ed. Grand Rapids: Baker, 2015.

———. *The Sin of Certainty: Why God Desires Our Trust More than "Correct" Beliefs.* New York: HarperOne, 2016.

Fea, John. *Believe Me: The Evangelical Road to Donald Trump.* Grand Rapids: Eerdmans, 2018.

Flannelly, Kevin, et al. "Beliefs about God, Psychiatric Symptoms, and Evolutionary Psychiatry." *Journal of Religion and Health* 49.2 (2010) 246–61.

Francis, Leslie. "God Images and Self-Esteem: A Study among 11–18 Year-Olds." *Research in the Social Scientific Study of Religion* 16 (2005) 105–21.

Fretheim, Terence. *God and the World in the Old Testament: A Relational Theology of Creation*. Nashville: Abingdon, 2005.

Froese, Paul, and Christopher Bader. *America's Four Gods: What We Say About God—and What That Says About Us*. New York: Oxford University Press, 2010.

———. "God in America: Why Theology is Not Simply the Concern of Philosophers." *Journal for the Scientific Study of Religion* 46.4 (2007) 465–81.

Galli, Mark. "Trump Should Be Removed from Office." *Christianity Today*, December 19, 2019. https://www.christianitytoday.com/ct/2019/december-web-only/trump-should-be-removed-from-office.html.

Gelfand, Michele, et al. "Differences Between Tight and Loose Cultures: A 33-Nation Study." *Science* 332 (May, 2011) 1100–1104.

———. "Trump Culture: Threat, Fear and the Tightening of the American Mind." *Scientific American*, April 27, 2016. http://www.scientificamerican.com/article/trump-culture-threat-fear-and-the-tightening-of-the-american-mind.

Giles, Kevin. *The Trinity and Subordinationism: The Doctrine of God & the Contemporary Gender Debate*. Downers Grove, IL: InterVarsity, 2002.

Glass, Jennifer, and Philip Levchak. "Red States, Blue States, and Divorce: Understanding the Impact of Conservative Protestantism on Regional Variation in Divorce Rates." *American Journal of Sociology* 119.4 (January 2014) 1002–46.

Gnuse, Robert. "Seven Gay Texts: Biblical Passages Used to Condemn Homosexuality." *Biblical Theology Bulletin* 45.2 (2015) 68–87.

Graham, Billy. "Interview." *Parade*, February 1, 1981, 6–7.

Gushee, David. *Changing Our Mind: A Call from America's Leading Evangelical Ethics Scholar for Full Acceptance of LGBT Christians in the Church*. 3rd ed. Canton, MI: Read the Spirit, 2017.

Heim, Joe. "Jerry Falwell Jr. can't Imagine Trump 'doing anything that's not good for the country.'" *Washington Post*, January 1, 2019.

Hetherington, Marc, and Jonathan Weiler. *Authoritarianism and Polarization in American Politics*. New York: Cambridge University Press, 2009.

———. *Prius or Pickup? How the Answers to Four Simple Questions Explain America's Great Divide*. Boston: Houghton Mifflin Harcourt, 2018.

Hugo, Victor. *Les Misérables*. Translated by Charles Wilbour. New York: Dutton, 1909.

Hydinger, Kristen, et al. "Penal Substitutionary Atonement and Concern for Suffering: An Empirical Study." *Journal of Psychology and Theology* 45.1 (2017) 33–45.

Jackson, Joshua, et al. "The Faces of God in America: Reveling Religious Diversity Across People and Politics." *PLoS ONE* (June 11, 2018). https://doi.org/10.1371/journal.pone.0198745

Jacobs, Tom. "Inside the Minds of Hardcore Trump Supporters." *Pacific Standard Magazine*, February 15, 2018. https://psmag.com/news/inside-the-minds-of-hardcore-trump-supporters.

Jankowki, Peter, et al. "Religious Beliefs and Domestic Violence Myths." *Psychology of Religion and Spirituality*. (March, 2018.) https://doi.org/10.1037/rel0000154.

Jankowski, Peter, and Stephen Sandage. "Attachment to God and Humility: Indirect Effect and Conditional Effects Models." *Journal of Psychology and Theology* 42.1 (2014) 70–82.

Jipp, Joshua. *Saved By Faith and Hospitality.* Grand Rapids: Eerdmans, 2017.

Johnson, Kathryn, et al. "Friends in High Places: The Influence of Authoritarian and Benevolent God-Concepts on Social Attitudes and Behaviors." *Psychology of Religion and Spirituality* 5.1 (2013) 15–22.

———. "The Mind of the Lord: Measuring Authoritarian and Benevolent God Representations." *Psychology of Religion and Spirituality* 7.3 (2015) 227–38.

Jones, Robert, et al. "Do Americans Believe Capitalism & Government are Working? Findings from the 2013 Economic Values Survey." The Brookings Institution, July 2013. https://www.brookings.edu/research/do-americans-believe-capitalism-government-are- working/.

Jost, John. "The End of the End of Ideology." *American Psychologist* 61.7 (October 2006) 651–67.

Kearney, Richard. *Anatheism: Returning to God after God.* New York: Columbia University Press, 2011.

King, Martin Luther, Jr. "Letter From a Birmingham Jail." 1963. https://www.africa.upenn.edu/Articles_Gen/Letter_Birmingham.html.

Kirkpatrick, Lee. "God as a Substitute Attachment Figure: A Longitudinal Study of Adult Attachment Style and Religious Change in College Students." *Personality and Social Psychology Bulletin* 24.9 (1998) 961–73.

Kirkpatrick, Lee, and Phillip Shaver. "An Attachment-Theoretical Approach to Romantic Love and Religious Belief." *Personality and Social Psychology Bulletin* 18.3 (1992) 266–75.

Krause, Neal, and Christopher Ellison. "Forgiveness by God, Forgiveness of Others and Psychological Well-Being in Late Life." *Journal for the Scientific Study of Religion* 42.1 (2003) 77–93.

Lakoff, George. *Don't Think of an Elephant! Know Your Values and Frame the Debate.* 2d ed. White River Junction, VT: Chelsea Green, 2014.

———. *Moral Politics: How Liberals and Conservatives Think.* Chicago: University of Chicago Press, 2002.

Lakoff, George, and Mark Johnson. *Philosophy in the Flesh.* New York: Basic, 1999.

Lamborn, Susie, et al. "Patterns of Competence and Adjustment Among Adolescents from Authoritative, Authoritarian, Indulgent, and Neglectful Families." *Child Development* 62 (1991) 1049–65.

Langston, Scott. *Exodus Through the Centuries.* Malden, MA: Blackwell, 2006.

Larzelere, Robert, et al. *Authoritative Parenting: Synthesizing Nurturance and Discipline for Optimal Child Development.* Washington, DC: American Psychological Association, 2013.

Levin, J. S. "Is Depressed Affect a Function of One's Relationship with God? Findings from a Study of Primary Care Patients." *International Journal of Psychiatry and Medicine* 32.4 (2002) 379–93.

MacArthur, John. "Does the Bible Permit a Woman to Preach?" https://www.youtube.com/watch?v=n8ncOf82ZJo&feature=youtu.be.

McConnell, Kelly, et al. Examining the Links Between Spiritual Struggles and Symptoms of Psychopathology in a National Sample." *Journal of Clinical Psychology* 62.12 (2006) 1469–84.

McGrath, Alister. *Reformation Thought: An Introduction.* 3rd ed. Oxford: Blackwell, 1999.

McKnight, Scot. *A Community Called Atonement.* Nashville: Abingdon, 2007.

Mockabee, Stephen. "A Question of Authority: Religion and Cultural Conflict in the 2004 Election." *Political Behavior* 29 (2007) 221–48.

Noll, Mark. *The Civil War as a Theological Crisis.* Chapel Hill, NC: University of North Carolina Press, 2006.

Olson, Roger. *Reformed and Always Reforming: The Postconservative Approach to Evangelical Theology.* Grand Rapids: Baker, 2007.

Pargament, Kenneth, et al. "God help me: Religious coping efforts as predictors of the outcomes to significant negative life events." *American Journal of Community Psychology* 18.6 (1990) 793–824.

———. "Religion and the Problem-Solving Process: Three Styles of Coping." *Journal for the Scientific Study of Religion* 27.1 (1988) 90–104.

Pepper, Miriam, et al. "A Study of Multidimensional Religion Constructs and Values in the United Kingdom." *Journal for the Scientific Study of Religion* 49.1 (2010) 127–46.

Pew Research Center. "When Americans say They Believe in God, What Do They Mean?" 2018. https://www.pewforum.org/2018/04/25/when-americans-say-they-believe-in-god- what-do-they-mean/.

Pinnock, Clark, et al. *The Openness of God.* Downers Grove, IL: InterVarsity, 1994.

The President's Task Force on 21st Century Policing. https://copsusdoj.gov/pdf/taskforce/taskforce_finalreport.pdf.

Prothero, Stephen. *The American Bible: How Our Words Unite, Divide, and Define a Nation.* New York: HarperOne, 2012.

———. *American Jesus: How the Son of God Became a National Icon.* New York: Farrar, Straus and Giroux, 2003.

———. *Why Liberals Win the Culture Wars (Even when they Lose Elections): How America's Raucous, Nasty, and Mean Culture Wars Make for a More Inclusive Nation.* New York: HarperOne, 2016.

Public Religion Research Institute. "Survey: A Shifting Landscape: A Decade of change in American Attitudes About Same-Sex Marriage and LGBT Issues." February 26, 2014. http://publicreligion.org/research/2014/02/2014-lgbt-survey/.

Putnam, Robert, and David Campbell. *American Grace: How Religion Divides and Unites Us.* New York: Simon and Schuster, 2010.

Rohr, Richard. *The Divine Dance: The Trinity and Your Transformation.* New Kensington, PA: Whitaker House, 2016.

Sample, Tex. *Working Class Rage: A Field Guide to White Anger and Pain.* Nashville: Abingdon, 2018.

Sandage, Steven, et al. "Calvinism, Gender Ideology, and Relational Spirituality: An Empirical Investigation of Worldview Differences." *Journal of Psychology and Theology,* 45.1 (2017) 17–32.

Sanders, John. *The God Who Risks.* Rev. ed. Downers Grove, IL: InterVarsity, 2007.

———. *No Other Name: An Investigation into the Destiny of the Unevangelized.* Grand Rapids: Eerdmans, 1992.

———. "Raising Hell about Razing Hell: Evangelical Debates on Universal Salvation." *Perspectives in Religious Studies* 40.3 (Fall 2013) 267–81. (A draft version is available at drjohnsanders.com.)

———. *Theology in the Flesh: How Embodiment and Culture Shape the Way We Think About Truth, Morality, and God.* Minneapolis: Fortress, 2016.

————. *What About Those Who've Never Heard? Three Views*. Downers Grove, IL: InterVarsity, 1995.

Sethi, Sheena, and Martin Seligman. "Optimism and Fundamentalism." *Psychological Science* 4.4 (1993) 256–59.

Shariff, Azim, and Ara Norenzayan. "Mean Gods Make Good People: Different Views of God Predict Cheating Behavior." *The International Journal for the Psychology of Religion* 21 (2011) 85–96.

Shen, Megan, et al. "Testing the *Love Thy Neighbor Hypothesis*: Religiosity's Association with Positive Attitudes Toward Ethnic/Racial and Value-Violating Out-Groups." *Psychology of Religion and Spirituality* 5.4 (2013) 294–303.

Sides, John. "How the United States Built a Welfare State for the Wealthy." *Washington Post* February 12, 2016.

Simpson, David, et al. "Understanding the Role of Relational Factors in Christian Spirituality." *Journal of Psychology and Theology* 36 (2008) 124–34.

Smith, Christian. *The Bible Made Impossible: Why Biblicism Is Not a Truly Evangelical Reading of Scripture*. Grand Rapids: Brazos, 2012.

Stark, Rodney. *The Triumph of Christianity: How the Jesus Movement Became the World's Largest Religion*. New York: HarperOne, 2011.

Stroope, Samuel, et al. "Images of a Loving God and Sense of Meaning in Life." *Social Indicators Research* 111.1 (2013) 25–44.

Taub, Amanda. "The Rise of American Authoritarianism." https://www.vox.com/2016/3/1/11127424/trump-authoritarianism.

Volf, Miroslav. *After Our Likeness: The Church as the Image of the Trinity*. Grand Rapids: Eerdmans, 1998.

————. *Exclusion and Embrace*. Nashville: Abingdon, 1996.

————. *Free of Charge: Giving and Forgiving in a Culture Stripped of Grace*. Grand Rapids: Zondervan, 2005.

Wallis, Jim. *America's Original Sin: Racism, White Privilege, and the Bridge to a New America*. Grand Rapids: Brazos, 2016.

Walton, John. *The Lost World of Genesis 1*. Downers Grove, IL: InterVarsity, 2009.

Webb, William. "A Redemptive Movement Model." In *Four Views on Moving Beyond the Bible to Theology*, edited by Gary Meaders, 215–48. Grand Rapids: Zondervan, 2009.

Welzel, Christian, and Ronald Inglehart. "Political Culture, Mass Beliefs, and Value Change." In *Democratization*, edited by Christian Haepfer, et al., 126–44. New York: Oxford University Press, 2009.

————. "Cultural Map." http://www.worldvaluessurvey.org/WVSContents.jsp.

Wiegand, Katherine, and Howard Weiss. "Affective Reactions to the Thought of 'God': Moderating Effects of Image of God." *Journal of Happiness Studies* 7 (2006) 23–40.

Wirzba, Norman. *Way of Love: Recovering the Heart of Christianity*. New York: HarperOne, 2016.

Wright, N. T. *Challenge of Jesus: Rediscovering Who Jesus Was and Is*. Downers Grove, IL: InterVarsity, 1999.

————. *The Day the Revolution Began: Rediscovering the Meaning of Jesus's Crucifixion*. New York: HarperOne, 2017.

————. *Jesus and the Victory of God*. Minneapolis: Fortress, 1996.

Zakaria, Fareed. *In Defense of a Liberal Education*. New York: Norton, 2015.

Zorwick, M. Leslie Wade. "Using Debate to Develop Perspective Taking and Social Skills." In *Using Debate in the Classroom*, edited by Karyl Davis et al., 107–16. New York: Routledge, 2016.

Made in the USA
Coppell, TX
09 February 2021